Dating

Find A Girlfriend or Boyfriend Who Is Faithful, Loyal & Supportive

(Learn How To Attract Men And Women and Make Them Fall In Love With You)

Blake Moreck

Published By **Andrew Zen**

Blake Moreck

All Rights Reserved

Dating: Find A Girlfriend or Boyfriend Who Is Faithful, Loyal & Supportive (Learn How To Attract Men And Women and Make Them Fall In Love With You)

ISBN 978-1-77485-800-4

No part of this guidebook shall be reproduced in any form without permission in writing from the publisher except in the case of brief quotations embodied in critical articles or reviews.

Legal & Disclaimer

The information contained in this ebook is not designed to replace or take the place of any form of medicine or professional medical advice. The information in this ebook has been provided for educational & entertainment purposes only.

The information contained in this book has been compiled from sources deemed reliable, and it is accurate to the best of the Author's knowledge; however, the Author cannot guarantee its accuracy and validity and cannot be held liable for any errors or omissions. Changes are periodically made to this book. You must consult your doctor or get professional medical advice before using any of the suggested remedies, techniques, or information in this book.

Upon using the information contained in this book, you agree to hold harmless the Author from and against any damages, costs, and expenses, including any legal fees potentially resulting from the application of any of the information provided by this guide. This disclaimer applies to any damages or injury caused by the use and application, whether directly or indirectly, of any advice or information presented, whether for breach of contract, tort, negligence, personal injury, criminal intent, or under any other cause of action.

You agree to accept all risks of using the information presented inside this book. You need to consult a professional medical practitioner in order to ensure you are both able and healthy enough to participate in this program.

Table of Contents

Chapter 1: Self Confidence 1

Chapter 2: How Do You Choose A Date? .. 8

Chapter 3: Master The Art Of Attraction 17

Chapter 4: How To Get His Attention 32

Chapter 5: Watch That Attitude, Young Lady! 43

Chapter 6: How To Approach A Girl You Aren't Sure Of And Impress Her 53

Chapter 7: The First Date 60

Chapter 8: Getting Ready 69

Chapter 9: How To Achieve Maximum Level Confidence 74

Chapter 10: First Date Tips 79

Chapter 11: Honesty/Vulnerability 89

Chapter 12: What Happens When Things Go Wrong 97

Chapter 13: Confidence, It's Vital 104

Chapter 14: Remember What You Text Your Girl 114

Chapter 15: One Night Stands 125

Chapter 16: How To Instantly Improve And Improve Your Game 133

Chapter 17: Keeping It Strong 138

Chapter 18: How To Face The Call To Agreement On The Date 152

Chapter 19: The Creep Factor And How To Avoid Being Misunderstood. 159

Chapter 20: You Are Not Always A Picnic. 171

Conclusion 183

Chapter 1: Self Confidence

It's important to be confident in your dating life. It is easy to feel negative about yourself. Be careful not to think that you can fool people. Men love confident women and vice versa. Confidence, which is a characteristic that women love most about a man, is described as one among the most sexiest traits he can possess. Males who lack self-confidence prevent them from being the successful men they desire in their relationship lives. You are usually your worst critic. And you might not realize it. You cannot expect others people to love and accept you unless you are able to do so.

Are you feeling bored? Are you willing to try out flirting? If you feel unsatisfied or have a bad sense of style, you may not be willing to go out much. Believe in yourself, if you want your appearance to be polished and attractive. You have to learn how to put your insecure thoughts to rest, not to allow them to interfere with your dating life.

If you believe that you don't possess the necessary qualities to find true love, you will not attract someone who is confident. Your success rate depends on how much confidence and self-assurance you have. Your whole experience will take on a negative tone if you keep a constant negative storyline running through your head. In addition to this, your partner will see the negative energy you are putting out. These things shouldn't bother you. The good news is you can become more confident. Faking it can help you get there. You will be able to become confident if you act like that confident you wish to be. When you feel at ease in your own skin, there is no way for anyone else to make you feel uncomfortable.

Being self-confident will improve your quality of life. This applies to your whole life and not just to your relationships. These are some ways to boost your confidence levels without sounding arrogant.

Do Things That You Love

Make a list if you are looking for activities that make people happy and content. Once you have a checklist, you can start to enjoy these activities more. Sometimes your environment or your way of spending your time can contribute to your lack of confidence. If you are unhappy in your job or surround yourself by people who do not add value, you can sink into negativity. Your perceptions and feelings about yourself will change based on the company you keep and how you spend time. People who are positive and driven will influence you.

Improve your Image

You will feel good if you look great. People who believed that appearances didn't matter were wrong. Your self-confidence and self-esteem will improve when you dress up. It is important to take time to maintain a well-groomed and professional appearance. Make sure you exercise regularly, eat healthy foods, and stay fit. If you improve your body image, the way that you feel about yourself will change.

Speaking

It is a smart idea to openly speak up about any personality traits you may have, such as shyness, introversion, or being reserved. If you know that you are a talkative person, then it is a good idea to start listening more than talking. It is vital to strike the right balance between being both a good listener as well as a speaker. You will find the middle and you should stick with it. Being able to tell the difference between speaking up and keeping your tongue down will bring you much joy in your daily life, and it will also help improve your relationship. This skill will demonstrate self-control, which can be translated into confidence. By doing so, you're essentially demonstrating that you can manage yourself and are assertive.

Eye Contact

Maintaining eye contact is crucial and it shows self-confidence. Do you keep eye contact while speaking? Do you look up at your partner or down at them while you are talking? Are you trying to keep eye contact but are unsure how? Eye contact matters because your eyes will always reflect how you feel. Looking someone in the eye can help you exude confidence. You don't need to stare at your date. All you need is to maintain eye contact every couple seconds.

Answering Questions

These are basic questions you can easily answer.

What do YOU do?

You might tell me a little bit about yourself.

What are you future plans and goals

What are YOU looking for?

These questions might be familiar to you a dozen or more times. However, very few people are able to give good answers. Spend some time to get a good answer. You should be able both to find good answers and to easily deliver them. If you take too many questions to answer, you may be uneasy about your life and the things you desire. Lack of self-assuredness can lead to low self-confidence. To make your date remember you, your answers should be entertaining and memorable. It is worth taking some time to contemplate them. If you are unable to, you might be able to collaborate with a friend and come up with some answers.

Revealing Yourself

Are you one of those people who stops to ask you what you want to do with your date when they ask you? If so, this can also be a sign you lack confidence. There is always time and a place for being cooperative, but it doesn't mean you have to be open-minded all the time. Let your dates learn about you, your hobbies, interests, likes, dislikes, and other aspects of your personality. It's okay for you to be open about your feelings, and it is best to feel confident about them.

Shush Your Inner Critic

You are your worst critic. Recognizing it is important will help you to improve yourself. The only thing that matters when you're on a date is to have fun and to make sure that she has a great time. Be aware of your inner voice, which may be telling you to stop doing something. Don't lose your confidence. Keep your eyes on the prize and focus on what is important. Your inner critic can critique you after the date, but not when you are actually on the date. You have the power over your thoughts, so try to stay in control.

Chapter 2: How do you choose a date?

Once you are aware of these three deceptive mistakes, we can focus the rest on your strategy for dating. Let me begin with the question.

What makes a good first date?

A good date is when you and a woman share an experience together that allows you both to discover your true selves. Let me elaborate.

The food is not what makes a good date. It is not about where you eat. It's not about what you spend on her. It is all about getting to know your partner and having fun. A woman is more concerned about participating in seeing the world. She wants you to be able to experience her as a person.

It's not hard to find a good date if you have positive vibes and are open to communication.

#1 - Positive vibes

If a woman does not feel happy from the first date, she is unlikely to want to stay with you. Why is it so common for first dates to fail? It's usually because she hasn't received positive vibes that show her that you are real and worth continuing to get to understand.

Some women sense when the words you use aren't in line with who you really think they are. As I stated before, many women can sense deceit as far away as a mile. If your partner can't detect deception, you will never be able to build a lasting relationship.

#2 - Open communication

When you first meet a woman for the first time, it is important to communicate openly. Women want to hear the truth about you, so it is important to communicate openly.

You can be confident about yourself and pursue open communication by being confident. You don't have to be convinced that you know what your life will look like. All you need to have the confidence to share your true self and your entire life. Women love honesty and confidence. It makes them feel safe.

Tips for a successful first date

To ensure a successful first date, you should follow these five tips.

#1 - Don't try and impress her

You know the deceitful error of acting like you're someone you aren't. The same deceptive strategy is used to charm a woman. One of two outcomes can be expected when you try to impress a lady.

First, gloating and bragging can be used to try to impress women. Confidence can be one thing but boasting about yourself is quite another. In order to impress her, you shouldn't brag about your past or present achievements. It's a huge turnoff and can bring you back to the beginning of good vibes.

Second, impressing a woman with your charm will give the impression that she is someone you aren't. Every person has been blessed with great moments. They aren't the best time to discuss them all. Don't tell a woman your greatest achievements during the first date. You can save them for another day.

When a personal achievement story is brought up, there are ways to communicate it without seeming boastful or trying to impress her. Honesty and open communication are key to impressing women. A woman can easily understand the words you say. You don't have to go overboard or be too sexy about explaining it.

#2 – Assume that she's already in you

You must assume that the woman in your relationship is already interested. Be open to the idea that your only purpose in this date is to get to learn more about her. Be clear that you're only deciding if and when you want to be with her. Your confidence will drop if you start thinking about whether or not she is interested in you. Focus on her when you go on your first date.

Although I am not suggesting that you should with a shadow of doubt believe she is into your, it can be hard to be surprised when she isn't. It is possible to be more confident when you don't believe her. It helps you get rid of your subconscious thoughts about impressing women. Your mind will tells, "She already likes my personality, so I don't need try to impress him with anything." Of course, it is possible for her to reject the information that you have about yourself. By assuming that she likes and trusts you, you can be confident and honest. That will bring you to a place of open communication.

#3 - Be honest with her

Honesty and open communication are the most effective forms of open communication. This is a great way to get along with women. Nobody likes being told lies and nobody enjoys having to withhold information from them. Being honest with your words, even when it isn't the most flattering, shows her that you are willing to share all information.

Let's say that you are sincere with a woman and share your past mistakes. A woman would rather hear your stories than hear them rehashing your mistakes. If you believe in yourself, you should be confident enough to not only explain the mistakes but also what you've learned. Make mistakes and learn from them. Honesty will move relationships forward. Ask any woman. Honesty will make you a better person.

#4 – Listen more than you speak

Talking too much is a fatal error that many men make. Even if the woman she is dating is extremely talkative, they will likely spend a lot more time talking to you than you. She wants to get acquainted with you. But, you must be able to stop talking.

Sometimes a woman just is too nice to stop talking and allow you the freedom to continue on with whatever topic you want. Here's an idea: If you find that you say or think, "Enough with me, how bout you?" then you, my friend are talking too loud.

Tip #2: Do you think she is already into me? This is the same as active listening. You are not trying to interview her for the boyfriend job. Instead, your goal should be to engage her in conversation.

Here's an example that can be used: Ask her one question. Listen to what she says. You're not "letting her talk", but instead focusing your attention on what she is saying. Too many men wait until a woman stops talking to them so they can speak about themselves. You have to be interested in what she is saying and how it is said. By asking follow-up questions regarding what she is talking about, you show that you are interested and active listener rather than waiting for her turn.

#5 - Do not expect anything to occur

This tip really summarizes all the others. I am not trying to impress her. However, being honest and open with her is the best way to expect nothing to happen.

You cannot expect a first date that ends in sex. Expecting a woman to touch you or show romance toward you is unreasonable. Expecting anything less than this is likely to lead you astray. Let me elaborate.

The first date might include romance. The first date could end in sex. She might even want to kiss and smear you. However, if you expect any one of these things, it is time to subconsciously employ tactics to get yourself in that position. Women can sense when you're trying for cues to get to bed. She can tell when you're trying for a kiss. All this does is make it appear that you're using forced tactics to ruin a wonderful conversation.

Instead of expecting anything, expect that she will like you. Your goal should be to be honest, open and confident. We will talk in a later chapter about cues to let you know she wants more. It is important to expect only open communication from your first date.

Finding the right first date is all in the exploration

You should only be on the first stage of exploration with a woman you are interested in dating. Trust me when you say that most women don't care about getting intimate with you from day one. They are more open to communication and will see things through. They want to know more about you, and they will explore you as a person. They don't need details about whether or not you like to kiss, or if your feelings for her are intimate. She wants to have a good experience with no drama and stress. Your environment should be stress-free and free from expectations. Things will move more quickly.

Chapter 3: Master The Art of Attraction

According to the evolutionary theory behind human attraction, we select romantic partners based in our evaluation of 'mate quality'. This is the person's romantic attractiveness based on their physical appearance and status.

This means your 'mate usefulness' will depend on your desirable or attracting qualities, habits, and traits. Mate value may be affected by your physical attractiveness as well as your intelligence and resources.

2.1. Whom Do you Want to Attract

Relax and think about the woman you want to share your life with. Clarity is power.

When I was struggling to relate to women, my goal became getting a woman or any woman. I began to improve my life and work on myself. Then, I saw that the women who came to see me were coming in droves.

I've also witnessed men just dating for the sake, without being specific about what their desires are. Without being specific, many men have seen women walk away from potential soul mates. To attract the woman you dream of and create a satisfying relationship, it is essential to first understand what you want.

Describe the qualities that you would like to see in your dream women

List the qualities you seek in your ideal women. This is not a complete list. Write down the ten most important qualities you want, and place them in an order that is convenient to you.

Here is an example of how you should move:

Honesty: This is something that I value most. It is why honesty ranks first on my list. The dishonesty of a woman, regardless of her beauty, is a huge turn-off.

Respectful. I can't love someone who doesn't value me, no matter her beauty. I love it when a woman looks back at me with admiration.

If you observe how women talk with their men, you can easily tell which woman holds them in high regard. I want a woman that treats others with respect.

A giver: It makes me happy when a woman thinks beyond the box and offers her help to her husband without him having to ask. It's hard to get along with someone who takes and gives without giving back as much as they get. I love someone who's a giver. I believe true love is a love for giving and not receiving. It's a turnoff for me when a woman feels that her beauty is all that matters, and that she has nothing more to offer in a relationship.

Communication is vital to a happy relationship. If a lady is unwilling to speak up and have honest conversations with me, it will turn me off.

Issues develop when couples fail to communicate. I admire women who openly share their emotions and voice what concerns them. I was once in a relationship that turned sour with a girl. It was really hard for her to come clean. Although you could see something was wrong from her actions, it was clear that she was not willing to talk in order to resolve any issues.

A person who is open-minded: I am an open-minded individual who is always looking for new experiences and learning more. When I see new ideas, they are welcomed and taken seriously. This is one reason why I have experienced a lot of growth in my own life. This is why I want a open-minded woman to come into my life.

Kindness is attractive to me. I love it when a woman shows affection, kindness, forgiveness, consideration, generosity, and is generous.

A caring person. I love a woman that is compassionate towards others. A woman who will give her time and care for others is in harmony with her feminine, nurturing nature.

I want a woman that is generous with her time and thoughtful for others.

Someone ambitious, passionate, & supportive: I am looking for a woman who supports me in my mission in life, is encouraging, and can add value to mine. In this context, value includes companionship, support, positive emotions (positive energy), admiration, and support.

Someone younger: I am much more attracted and attracted than my age to younger women. At least 5, 6, or even more years younger that me.

Someone beautiful. I have done a lot over the years on myself. This includes better dressing and grooming, improving my physique, better financial lives, etc. I'd also like a woman who takes care and isn't afraid to take care of her health or emotional well-being.

Someone who is easygoing. I don't want someone that gets mad at the slightest provocation. Or who isn't willing to fix relationship issues as they arise. I want a understanding, patient and forgiving lady.

When you have written down the qualities you want to see in your dream woman's character, you can place this list anywhere you like every day. It is important to be focused on what you want. According to many universal laws, such as the law that attracts, you attract those qualities into your life.

Your list should not be thrown away. You can focus on it each day so you can gain clarity. Next, write your love letter to the person you haven't yet met. As you write this letter, picture yourself in complete love with this person. Send her everything you love about this person in your letter. It is best to write the letter as if this were a letter you would send to someone who is already in love with you. Here, the goal is to visualize yourself attracted by your ideal lady even before it happens. Get started now and do this exercise. Be vulnerable and let your heart speak.

2.2. Attract the person that you are meant to be

After writing a love letter and creating a list, be honest about yourself about your characteristics. "Like attracts like" is essentially the motto of life.

It is impossible for a lazy, unmotivated man to desire an ambitious, driven woman who takes care herself. Some men who are dishonest claim that they want an honest partner. A woman who is good at communication is desirable by some men. If a woman is confident, attractive and dedicated to her personal growth and taking care of herself, she will be attracted by a man who has the same qualities.

Your goal should always be to attract people. Be the person you wish to attract. Work to develop a positive trait in yourself that you are lacking.

For instance, if your list of quality includes a woman who is well-groomed and takes care to herself, but your inner self is not in the best place, then you should start to work on yourself. If you want a caring, selfless woman but are not inclined to give, then you should embark on the journey of becoming a giver.

You can look at your current list and see the areas that you need improvement. It all starts with you.

Are you a fan of couples that share similar values and have you ever seen them together?

It is important to remember that such relationships are not just happenstances. When you learn about these couples, you'll discover that their shared characteristics are what brought them together in the first place.

If you are not clear about your goals and don't have a clear vision of what you desire, it will be hard to attract the right woman. Unfortunately, many men fail to clarify their wants, which is probably why today's society is filled with couples who aren't aligned in values, as well as many people who have unhealthy and unhappy relationships.

Most people have career goals. Few people set goals for relationship, which is an inexplicable thing as relationships are such a vital area of life.

The choice of which woman to spend your entire life with is a significant one. It can bring you pleasure or pain. Unfortunately, many men rush to make this choice due to society pressures or fear. It is not uncommon for men to say "Hey my friends are getting married." I should get married also." Some men settle for women they don't like, or because they fear the consequences. Fear is a reason to avoid a life partner.

Neil Strauss said the following: "Perhaps I made the biggest mistake in my life, believing that love was about finding someone. The truth is that love is about finding the right one. The person you choose to spend the rest of your life with is not who you look for. Make the choice to live with the person you love.

If you are ready to become the woman you dream of spending your life with, invest in yourself. If you do this, you will attract the right kind of woman. This principle is what leads to passionate, loving relationships. They are easygoing, deep and mutually beneficial. These men are the type people look at and say, "These two have an amazing relationship."

2.3. Get away from the desire to have someone in your life

Attraction can be destroyed by neediness, desperation, and neediness. Becoming desperate and dependent is a huge turnoff. Do not be dependent on her if she is going to reject you. Don't get too attached to the idea of having your girlfriend or wife. It's time to let go of the attachment. Attachment to a relationship can hinder your ability to attract the woman that you desire. Attachment to a partner or a relationship can make you less attractive.

The common belief in our society today is that to be happy, you need women or to get married. This is far from the truth. Do not try to attract women who will make your life happy. Be happy first. If you wait for a woman that will make your life better, you'll be miserable for the rest of your life. Women don't want to fix men. Your happiness is yours.

Find the right partner for you (the process mentioned above). But, live your best life with a single man. Keep living your life to the fullest and making memories. Enjoy your hobbies and live a purposeful existence.

I had a friend who was extremely good with women. I noticed that his approach towards dating was a bit sloppy and unattached. He didn't want to focus on dating only one woman. He was more interested in dating many women. He found that the more he dated women after another, the more women wanted him. After questioning why it was so, I realized it was because he was from a place that was rich.

Women are attracted to men who have options for other women. It is important not to be too obvious. Her view is that having options indicates you're a great fish. This has been true of me. One time I was with someone who didn't initially interest me. However, once she saw me walking and talking with other women, some just friends, her attraction for my increased and she started calling me and texting.

You can meet more women as a single guy by talking to and meeting more of them. When you become your "girlfriend", when you're in love, or when one of the women becomes your girlfriend, don't be too focused on her.

Your goal is to practice your communication skills and interact with women. So when you do finally meet the woman that you desire, your conversations will flow naturally and you will seem confident and attractive. Confident men attract women. Many women will reject men who lack confidence or are easily intimidated.

Nothing says "I'm confident" like being passionate and purposeful. The next chapter focuses on the importance and value purpose in attracting a woman to your life and establishing a satisfying relationship.

2.4. Simple Strategies that Will Make You A More Attractive Men

Use the strategies below

Your body needs to be taken care of

The attraction guide is a book, so naturally, one must have attractive bodies.

However, it is not the way to attract women.

You should be focusing on your body and not just about your abs. Your level of attractiveness will increase if you work out in a way which pushes you beyond your comfort zone.

Make it funny

Humor is mentioned throughout the book several times. Humor is an important part of many aspects dating and relationship. Humor is a great attraction factor, but it's not as important as confidence. Marilyn Monroe was spot on when she stated that "If a woman can laugh, it's possible to make her do anything."

The funny thing about men trying to be funny or witty is that they fail. Laughter and joy can never be faked. Instead of trying to be convincing or giving her the perfect personality, make it real. Engage with her and show genuine interest.

It's a great way for her to laugh and have fun. You could take something she says, and twist it into something funny. She will be happy if you do this with a smile and a good attitude.

Avoid pickup lines

Pickup lines indicate a man trying too hard to impress women. Pickup lines are not for confident men, especially ones that are too cheesy. These men engage women and have meaningful conversations.

Chapter 4: How to Get His attention

After spending some time playing the numbers games on Tinder or other dating apps, the next step should be to try and get the attention of the right man. It's important to pay attention to the following tips. Otherwise it's all too easy to get lost in your own thoughts. It's easy just to turn wrong and attract the wrong person again. They might be different in their jobs and identities but they're the same person. Here's the way you can do it.

You need to keep your eyes on the type and number of guys you will be able to date. As I have said, you've made a decision to stay focused on the types and men that you're attracted to.

I know there are many nice-looking men out. Many are easy-going. There are many smooth talkers. However, if you are not attracted to this type of man, then don't get distracted. Next, it is important to focus your attention on the type of men you selected in Chapter 1. This is where a bit of research comes in. You must get to know them. What kind values would they choose? What kind of interests might they have? Knowing these facts you should be able figure out the kind of signals that they would seek.

You need to know what he is interested in. For example, if a man is competitive, it is likely that he is into sports, or any other activity that involves a lot.

It is vital that you take the time to develop a psychological profile of what type of man you desire to attract. As much as you like, you can trace the path from the personality type to which you would like to attract the person to your possible interests. This is all speculation and guesswork. But it's better that just hoping or praying.

However, creating a random profile to post on the Internet is a surefire way to get lucky. Nine out ten times you'd attract the wrong man if you used the incorrect bait.

This reminds you of the many men who complain about not being able to attract gold diggers. These guys have three main ways of attracting women. They drive a BMW, wear Armani clothes and have lots of gold jewelry to go to gold digger night clubs. It is easy to connect the dots. You can simply say that the type of bait used will affect the kind and species of fish you catch. If you are using dollar bills, you can expect hippies to not be attracted. But, if you use gold diggers, they will. Women are also affected by the same.

To attract an intelligent, passionate, vision-oriented, and ambitious man, it's important to understand his interests and get to know him. Don't post photos of you naked. You will be surprised at the type and quality of men you attract.

It's essential to get inside the heads of your target audience.

Make a profile theme

Different people are attracted by different themes. A man who values the arts will seek out free spirits, for example. Many men who are interested in philosophy and compassionate volunteering prefer a certain theme. An individual who volunteers at a soup pantry or at the Peace Corps might be able to attract their attention. It's amazing how this works.

Take a look at the type of men you are interested and see what themes they would like to explore. This is especially true if you are ambitious. Many men fall into one of two camps. They either are drawn to the looks and looking for trophy partners or are looking for someone who can help them build an empire. In other words, they want a woman who is as ambitious and driven as them.

It is important that you identify the common themes people gravitate towards. It is obvious that this is speculation. However, this is better than trying to create a product that people would like and then attracting all the scumbags.

Make a random profile if your goal is to be used or abused. There are many attractive men out there. To find the right men for you, you must be more methodical, systematic and deliberate.

The secret is to start!

You must take action on any large project in your life. It may sound obvious but it is true that many people would prefer to purchase a book. I know that your goal is to solve all your problems. It won't make your problems disappear by reading my book. You have to put this information into action.

I am a selfhelp author. I have written many self-help book and unfortunately, I haven't found one that works. It won't make your man problems disappear by just reading the Kindle book. You must start. You must act. I felt the need to dedicate a section to this issue because many people believe that gathering information, talking with people, and spending some time online or social media is actually taking action. No, they're not. They are wasting our time.

Analyse paralysis can happen in many cases. This is the stage where you keep asking for more data. This is not a good situation for dating. You're simply sending out your profile, and then collecting responses from men. You're not trying to filter them. They aren't going to be contacted. You're just sitting around collecting information.

I am sorry but you have got to get off of the fence. The only way to resolve your problems is to pull the trigger. Don't let your analysis paralysis overtake you.

Analysis paralysis stops you from finishing a profile. I've seen this happen a lot. Some women, who may be intelligent, attractive, and very attractive, are afraid to leave out certain details or change their mind about what kind of profile they create.

It's important to recognize that perfection will never be achieved. There is always improvement. You have to make the right choice today. Tomorrow is not today. You must decide when you will finish your profile. Keep in mind that it will not be perfect. There will always be some areas that could use improvement but you need to accept the fact that there are still parts of your work to do.

Another thing that I noticed when it came to dating profiles was that people would change their profile often every few weeks. Even if they are attracting men to it, they would continue changing it because they feel it's insufficient.

I ask you to stay clear of both these situations. Make a timeline for the completion of your profile. Stick to it. Do not hesitate to create a profile that reflects the niches you are interested in.

Maximum attention is required by testing, testing and testing

Now that you have finished your profile, you can publish the profile and start to attract men. The good news: despite the fact that mobile dating apps have a very low ratio of women to men, it is possible to attract tons of people. The problem is getting the right eyes.

Women can get very desperate at this stage. They go through their profiles and make changes. They either think they are fat or say the wrong thing. Modifying your profile requires a lot of planning. It's just like selling online.

Professional online merchants have a process of improving their ads. They don't make random changes depending on how they feel the next day. They have a set process they follow to improve the effectiveness and reach their marketing materials. The same strategy is required for you. How? By resolving and testing your profile in the right way, you can get the right eyeballs.

The best way to approach things is to be methodical and systematic. The wrong way is to act in desperate circumstances. So, out of random inspiration, your profile is taken apart, the photos and texts are changed, and you just hope for better. That isn't testing. This is called gambling. I hope that you can tell the difference.

The best system Go elemental!

Professional online marketers can change their marketing creativity in a very systematic fashion, as I already mentioned. Elemental is one of most powerful and simple ways to improve your online dating profile.

If you look at your profile, you'll see that there are many parts to it. Here we are referring to your headline, title, photo, biography text, interests, location and even the area you live. These are not random details. You can adjust them.

The trick is to tweak only one element at time. This is how elemental design works. You go element by element. Your picture is the obvious place to start. This is an essential element. Try changing your profile picture, running it again and seeing if that changes your results.

Once you've made an improvement you can now move on to the next part of your profile: the headline or title. You can modify it until you get even more results.

Once you have achieved the best results, you can move on the next element. This is your biography.

Knowing when it is time to stop tweaking you profile

It is not as exciting as optimizing your profile for dating can be. However, the benefits will eventually diminish. You will never see an improvement in your results, no matter how diligently you optimize your dating profile. You have reached an end point. Although you might still see some incremental gains, it is not worth the effort.

It is essential to know when to quit. Consider stopping when the men you're attracted aren't growing in any meaningful way. I don't mean very minor upward ticks. These are not substantial increases. Once you have reached that stage, you are able to stop optimizing and changing your dating profile.

Chapter 5: Watch That Attitude, Young Lady!

But you know the best part? It doesn't matter if you are the hottest person in the world, but it won't suffice unless your attitude is right. As you may have heard, attitude is everything. I, like many others, would argue that attitude is more powerful when it come to attraction than physical appearance. A polished, elegant demeanor will make up the majority of your perceived sins.

What is the right attitude? What makes men lust after a women and what behavior would make her irresistible to a man's eyes? Is she to be timid? Are you more assertive or coy? Can she give him the reins or should she signal her willingness?

According to a well-known meme, "Why don't they have both?"

Research shows that men prefer it when you give them the reins and let them decide. You are also considered very sexy by men when they approach you. This is great news. It is clear that there is no right nor wrong. So why not consider both of these options?

1. Being passive

Pros:

It allows him be the man of authority and feels masculine. He tries to seduce and woo your heart.

He is responsible for all the effort, not you.

You have the advantage to be able learn from his behaviour and adjust your own behavior accordingly

You are in control. You can say yes/no without hurting anyone.

Cons:

It limits your choices to only the men who are willing to approach or approach you

Sometimes you may find yourself waiting all night for the right man to talk to you

2. Being aggressive

Pros:

You decide who you like best and you can approach the man of your choice

Being the guy who goes up to a guy and hits on him can be very liberating.

Some guys are very attracted to women with the courage to approach them.

You have the final say in the night. You don't need to wait for some guy who isn't there.

Cons:

There are men who are offended or feel humiliated by women who "steal the thunder" and make the first move.

It's your job to strike up a conversation, make a good hook and win him over.

You could be subject to rejection. This could not only harm your ego but also make it more difficult for you depending on the level of disrespectful behavior displayed by the guy.

It is a matter both of your personal preferences and that of men. Some women simply don't want to wait for Prince Charming. Others prefer to keep it safe and make him work for it. After all, you're worth it, right?

Confidence

My next point is now. This is the conclusion of all my discussions: confident people, especially males, are what we like. Confident girls are the best. Why shouldn't we? The one thing we seem to all be lacking is confidence. We can't help but admire the traits of a magical unicorn, male or woman, and feel attracted to them. What do confident girls look like to a guy?

For one, she is self assured. This girl doesn't need constant reassurance. She's not looking for validation from a man.

She is independent. A confident girl is independent. She doesn't have to be dependent on him, which makes it all the more appealing because he can lose her at any given moment.

She is very cool. This woman is clearly too cool, interesting, and she is just plain fascinating to him. She has many friends and interests. She can also lead a normal life with her own independence. He's simply with us for the ride, and he loves it all.

So, what can you do? How can confidence be made so that you can charm and seduce men to the point of obsession? Here are some useful tips:

Work on your self-esteem

This is an all-encompassing problem that doesn't just affect women. Many women experience low self-esteem. It can be caused by internal conflicts or body image issues. "Learning to love yourself" is not the best advice. Instead, let me list some ways you can boost your self-esteem.

Your environment should be filled with positive messages. Begin your day with something kind to you in the mirror. Pay attention to what your friends say about you. This positive affirmation will gradually improve your outlook.

Do something to improve your self-esteem. This is no excuse to be unhappy! If you don't love something about yourself, there are two options. You either learn to accept it, or you can make changes. I encourage you to embrace your personality, flaws and body. But, you can't deny that a minor change, like changing your haircolor, could make you happier or make yourself feel more beautiful. I'm a big believer in self-improvement.

Be confident in your appearance

You want to know what makes women irresistible? Feeling irresistible. A feeling of being beautiful, sexy or empowered can boost your attraction. It's obvious that people will see your low self-esteem and will not be attracted to you if you feel unattractive.

Before you go, choose your favorite song, pick your best outfit (the one that makes you look fabulous), then get out there. Feeling confident about yourself will make you radiate confidence. This is the right time to capitalize and get down on that cutie staring at you. It's possible!

Put your nervousness into practice.

It is possible to be insecure about your interactions with men. Take a moment to reflect on this. Is it their intimidation? Do you find that it is difficult to strike up a conversation with someone or to find the right topic? Or perhaps it's flirting that makes people nervous. Whatever you fear, practice is key. It means that if enough practice is done, you will not only become a pro but also be able power through the problem without any problems.

You could, for example, seek the support of a male friend so you can discuss appropriate topics with the other sex, flirting strategies, etc. This will allow you to get feedback on your "performance" and also give you some advice from the "inside". It is easier to master the skill when you have someone to help you.

Relaxation

A relaxed person is easier to approach and is more welcoming than one who is under pressure, I think. While you may not notice it, people around you can easily tell if someone is feeling comfortable or not. It's not only because of your expression, but also because our bodies release stress hormones when we are stressed. Your body language, your demeanor, as well as your body language, can reflect your mood. This can make it difficult to meet potential suitors. However, that is precisely what we don't need. So, how can we resolve this problem? Relax.

You can see the difference between a relaxed person and someone who is stressed by their behavior. A happy woman will be cheerful, positive, and open to social interaction. An unhappy woman will be more focused on her own problems. Let's discover how to signal that you're calm and "open for business".

Smile! Smile! It's not a good idea to be a Debbie Downer. Instead, smile wide and flirt with your eyes. Eye contact + smile = sure target.

Pay attention to how you move. Let's say a woman is sitting in a dark corner and her shoulders are hunched. Her arms are crossed over her chest. She isn't happy. Now imagine a smiling woman with no physical barriers between the people she loves and the people around. She is present, pointing her eyes at her conversation partner, and appears to be having the time she wants. Which woman do YOU think is more approachable and friendly? Which woman (or male) would it be more appealing to you? I think I've made it clear.

Don't be afraid to have a conversation. Many women find that it is difficult to talk about their feelings. It can make it difficult to go out with guys and might even keep you from dating. But, it's up to you to maintain a conversation. It takes two people tango. Also, it takes two people for a conversation. Don't get discouraged.

Talk to him about yourself. Ask questions about him about himself.), flirt a little, etc. If you feel the conversation is dragging on, don't panic. Sometimes silence is okay.

Chapter 6: How To Approach A Girl You Aren't Sure Of And Impress Her

1. Take a look at it

If she is not looking at you, tell her. Pay attention to her movements and keep your distance if she draws your attention. You will attract her attention and make her wonder if she is actually watching you.

2. Visually connect

When she spots you, take a moment to glance at her before turning away. Keep checking her out occasionally. Every so often, stop looking at her and look away. Doing so will make her feel attractive. You might not get a response, but she may not be inspired by your actions. Eye to eye communication is an important tool when you're trying to figure out how to move towards a young girl.

3. Feel constrained, but off-kilter

Assuming that your companions are nearby, take a look at your companions now. You don't want to seem distracted or not interested in the conversation being had with them. That will help her to see that you have her in your thoughts, and not just your own. This is sweet and inconspicuous!

4. Grin at her

Keep eye contact with your partner once in awhile, just a few times at a time. When you feel confident, smile briefly from the side of her lips and let her know. A big smile is not the best thing for her.

These actions help build the relationship and let her know you are interested in her. If she is genuinely interested in you, you will be able to better understand the situation. If she responds to your signals in a comparatively way, it could indicate that she is eager to have conversations with you.

If she does start to neglect you at any time, it is likely she will not be interested in you.

5. For the moment, you will be able to determine how to make a move towards a young girl.

Sometimes you can just trust that the young girl will allow you to have a conversation with her. If she's genuine interested in you and desires to chat with you about it, she would open the doors for you. She could walk alone to the women's area, ignore her companions and make a call or simply smile at you before leaving.

It's easier to communicate with a young lady if she is alone. There are no interruptions by her companions or abnormal minutes, since she is as of now anticipating that it's time to move towards you.

6. The gestures you should use to communicate with her

You can make sure that you are noticed by using the right motions. Although it is difficult, once you communicate your ideas, the idea will be able to take root as long as it is done well.

Gaze directly towards her, and smile. Once you have locked eyes with each other, tilt your neck just a bit so that your head is in line. Next, use your eyes to direct her towards the exit or counter. Whatever happens, she will see what you mean, and you can get to the point you were pointing at with no one else.

Although not all young girls will appreciate your motioning at them and asking for their attention, she may be open to the idea of you talking with her.

7. The test – She's in a group of young ladies

Keep your eyes on her and approach with confidence. Move forward into the crowd but look straight toward her. Any other person you see will be a jealous observer and they'll make rude comments to you since you didn't pick them as playmates.

"Hello... I do not intend to interfere with the young ladies. However, I could talk to you briefly. I really won't have the chance to excuse me in the unlikely event that I left the spot without getting more acquainted with you...

It doesn't matter what line you choose, it will still work so long as it is not mangled. However, it is important to make her feel uncomfortable by saying something which reveals how serious she needs to know you. If her companions seem to agree with your position, such as by poking her at you or smiling broadly, try to not take a look at them. You are only asking for trouble.

8. Ask about whether you could get her a drink

This works well in bars, provided that you can effectively get her to look up and stir it. The server will offer to bring her the same beverage as she is now drinking. The server might drop a funny and great message, such as "The courteous man sitting there might like to offer your this beverage...

You will know when she is ready to acknowledge the beverage and then look towards you smiling. She will see you as a weakling if you stand around too long. If you don't get her a drink before building the association, you will make it look like you are an unpleasant person.

9. If there are two young girls in a crowd,...

Walking with only two young ladies in your group, you can depend on them and still look at the young lady. If the young lady seems to be interested in you, she will allow her companion to go along unobtrusively and with a reason. But, no matter what the companion does, it is important to present yourself as a person and to say something nearly identical to the line in the third point. Keep the young lady's companion in mind for this discussion. It will also help her to have an honest view of herself. Be that though, it's important to keep your attention on the young lady!

These are the best discussion moves to remember. However, keep in mind that you must ensure that it works consistently. Create the pressure with your eyes and your eye contact connection first. It's a common occurrence to charm the young lady before you approach.

Chapter 7: The first date

Here are some things to remember

Do you text her? Do you invite her to coffee or for drinks? Do you feel you should talk more or less? Sometimes it can be difficult to know the intricacies about dating. You'll find tried and tested tips for dating that will work for everyone in this section.

Be personable

You must be friendly. If you are asking a woman to go out on a first date, don't text, or worse, send her an email. Email and texts can be impersonal forms to communicate. It's a great way to get to know someone by asking them out on a date. To ask her out on a date, you can pick up the telephone and call her. It sets the tone for communication and a healthy relationship.

Slow down

Online dating has a tendency to bring with it some risk and anxiety. You should spend time getting acquainted with your date online. Once you reach a certain level, you can invite her to meet you in person. It is important to take it slow.

Initiative

Before you go out with someone, make sure you have some great ideas for places to take her on a first date. Don't leave the planning and decision-making to the woman. You can avoid situations such as "Where would you like to go?" It is important to have a few choices. Women are attracted to men who can be decisive. Set a date with her and tell her the time and whereabouts. Do it confidently and it is very unlikely she will say no.

You should make sure she feels safe. This should be a priority. Unless your lady suggests otherwise you should ensure that the first few dates are in public areas and that you drive separate.

Your comfort

Men believe that they are being gracious and gentlemanly when they let the woman decide where the date is held. Women prefer men who can be in control, as we've already mentioned. You must suggest a familiar place and one you feel comfortable with. It is only by making someone feel comfortable that you can make them feel comfortable. You shouldn't suggest a sushi eatery if you don't enjoy sushi.

Confirm

Don't you confirm your doctor or dentist appointment? Why not do the exact same thing for your date? You can call her to confirm the date. It will confirm your date is correct and make you feel more at ease.

Make sure that your car is clean

If you are taking her out for a ride in the car, she must make sure that it is clean before you allow her to take it on your first date. Impression are important to women. This includes cleanliness. A girl will take a look at your car, and base their decision on how you manage your daily life.

Cash

Check with a cashier before you go to the venue to ensure that you have enough money in order to pay for parking, food, and any other expenses.

Dress comfortably

It shows respect that you have taken the time to dress up and look good. If you're wearing a band shirt with old jeans, it is a signal that you believe you should be there.

Let her Know What to Expect

You should make sure that your date knows where you are going to be and what you will do. Most men don't take the time to think about what clothes they will wear and how they will appear, until just before they go to pick up their girlfriend. Women, on other hand, are more likely to anticipate what they will wear and how it will look so they can prepare and take the time to get ready. It's important to let her know ahead of time where you'll travel so that she can dress appropriately for the destination. You can make women uncomfortable by not dressing appropriately for the situation.

The Date

Step 1: Picking your Date

The first step of any date includes picking up the date. Here are the rules for picking up your date.

Being on Time

To pick her up, make sure you arrive on time. Being late to the date can be a sign that the man doesn't value her time and could even cause her anxiety about the night ahead. If there is a reason that you will be late to the date, let her know.

Come up to her Door

It's possible that the cool guys will pull up at their date's door and honk her horn to grab her attention. However this is not a movie. Instead of texting, honking, or even honking, you should walk up to her house. It is the most gentlemanly thing to do in this circumstance and shows that your care.

She will be gratified

Every time you see her, be sure to compliment her. A majority of girls are meticulous about their appearance before meeting their first date. Make sure you give her a compliment. Don't be afraid to praise someone.

Step 2 What to do on the Day?

This may sound like a great way to go, but you should not take your date to a movie. We have already said that the main purpose of a date is for you to get to know your date. Your first date should feel romantic, fun, casual, and light.

Include walking

It's a great idea to walk in your first date. It's easier to be with someone if you're walking along the riverside or in a museum. This gives you the opportunity to communicate freely with your fellow travelers and helps you share your ideas. If you do decide that you want to go to dinner after the meeting, you will have already broken ice.

Pay

To get your first date, you must adhere to the old custom of paying for the date. This is the only acceptable option, unless your are Dutch. It proves that chivalry has not died. Although she might be willing to help, don't allow her to cover it.

Step 3

The date is not yet set; it is important to make sure everything runs smoothly well after the date.

Get her up

Once the date is over and you are done, you can go back up to her home and make sure she enters safely. Try to make eye contact with her as you walk up to her house. This is a polite but non-threatening way to establish contact and observe her reactions.

Can you kiss her? Can you make a play for her? There is no one-size fits all approach to this issue. It all depends on the atmosphere and how the evening went. You need to remember that some people don't consider kissing meaningful. It is okay to have a second chance if she has expressed interest. It is possible for her to ask you to bring her in, but your refusal will build anticipation and drive you wild.

Goodbye Kiss

Perhaps the most important thing for men on their first date, is the goodbye kiss. Let it happen naturally and don't try to force it. You might find your date uncomfortable kissing you or feeling awkward. If that is the case you can ask for a second date or put off the kissing until later. Before you reach for her cheeks and kiss her, make sure that she is sending the same signals to you. Simple idea: kiss her cheek gently and then turn your back. Go in for the kiss, even if her eyes close or she leans forward. If she moves backwards or turns her face away from you, this is probably not the best time to kiss.

These tips will ensure you make a great impression on your first date. It's important to make the date go smoothly so you can quickly get out on another date.

Chapter 8: Getting ready

The nature of your date is a great way to prepare. You need to be prepared for any type of date, whether blind date, double date or casual. You don't want your date to see you in the wrong clothes, wearing too much make up, or simply looking silly because you didn't think about it. That's the last impression you want. How can you avoid this catastrophe? Get ready for that date.

Be a man or woman, regardless of gender, before you go out on a date, it is important to feel good. Your mood will make or break the whole night. Remember that your partner expects you to have a good time, and you should too. Make sure you make your date's day more fun by setting a positive mood.

It is essential to get enough sleep before going on a date. Dinner time is the most important part of most dates. You must have both completed the day's tasks before you can go to your date. Either one of you or both may have been feeling exhausted by work and all that you have done on that day. You can take a quick power-sleep to rest your body and keep you energized for that day. The minimum amount of time you need to nap is 30 minutes. It's important to take some time to unwind and relax. This will allow for you to have the energy and motivation needed to make your date a success.

To get the best mood for your date, take a bath if you have time. Showers can be a stress-relieving activity for some. It can relieve your body and relax your entire body. This will help to relieve any muscle tension your date might experience. Plus, you will look fresh on the date. Plus, it will make you look fresh when you go on that date.

Also, if you want to make your date night successful, it will help you smell amazing. If you want to attract your partner, make sure that you smell good. It's key to how you experience things. The power and versatility of scent can be tricky. It can be tricky, but if done correctly, this will make your partner swoon over the way you smell. It is like branding your self with a smell. You can make your mark by using your scent.

Preparing your outfit in advance of your date is a good idea to avoid panicking and making a mess. Also, this will make you look good to your date. Be proud of the way you dress during your date. That does not mean you have to be perfect for the date. It is important to look professional so that your date can hit the ground running.

The casual dress code for guys is to wear button down polo tops and pants. Do not wear shorts and a standard tshirt. This will make you appear as if you just walked out of your house. You want to look both elegant and stylish. You can make your professional appearance more professional by wearing closed shoes such sneakers or leather shoes.

The best way to dress down for girls is with casual dresses or cute skirts with nice tops. Avoid looking like a slut or someone who just wants to flirt and have flings with you. If you feel the need to wear heels, opt for flats or sandals. Avoid wearing flip flops with your date.

To brighten your face for girls, you can use a little make-up. Apply just enough makeup to make you face stand out. A light gloss or blush can help you achieve that look. Remember that it is make up, not wet painting. So be careful when applying make-up to your face on dates.

Also, your hair should be part of the preparation zone for the date. Your hair should be neat and tidy all evening. If you are out with men, a straight-cut would be the best. Don't put hair in your food! Any hairstyle will do for girls as long that it isn't too messy or overdone. Do not make it look like your are performing in a concert. Both of you should remember to brush your hair regularly and keep it neat, so it can add professionalism to the professional look you want.

Even with all the preparation you do for your special day, have fun. Because you deserve it. Don't let the preparation for a date become a burden. You should actually enjoy it. Do not put pressure on your date by feeling stressed out or anxious. This will only make the date feel less relaxed. To ensure that you don't interfere with your evening, do not think too much about the things you are doing to prepare for your date. Relax and enjoy your first date. You'll be more successful on your second.

Chapter 9: How To Achieve Maximum Level Confidence

Confidence is important, as confidence is what people like to be around. Your chances of meeting women with confidence are bound to increase. Improvements in your life will help you feel more confident. Here are some things you can do:

1) Train a lot. You can go to the gym and lift weights, or you can do cardio. Scientifically, working out can make you happier. If you continue to work out, you will be in good shape.

2) Eat healthy meals. People who are overweight, lazy, or unhealthy will feel less satisfied than those who eat well and take care of their bodies.

3. Find a hobby, and get good at it. Spend some time working on your hobby if you aren't good at it. Because you are supposed to be doing something useful, having a hobby

makes you happier. It will also make your life more interesting. A hobby can help you become more competitive, which in turn will increase your confidence.

Dress well. Being confident will increase your self-esteem. If you're confident enough to be noticed at a social gathering, even though you may not be the most well-dressed, it will help you feel more confident.

5) Never base decisions on what people think about you. Do not listen to anyone criticizing your music taste. Confident people aren't interested in what other people do.

6) Be successful. Being successful can make you feel like an evilass. See how even the most average-looking people attracted women.

7) Find friends to make yourself feel better.

8) Keep a positive relationship to your family. This will make you happier.

9) Be ambitious. It is a way to feel purposeful and achieve your goals. Your ambition will make your life great.

10) Get adequate sleep every night. Sleep is crucial. If you aren't getting enough sleep, your energy levels and positivism will drop. Lacking enough sleep will make it harder to pursue your goals, get fit, exercise and have fun with your friends. You can make your confidence grow by setting goals and making friends.

11) Get rid negative people from you life. Negative people have been shown to cause you to feel unhappy.

12) Take a look at funny TV shows and movies. It will help you to feel more happy.

13) When you want something to occur, do it. Don't look for excuses. Just do it. When you make things happen, you become more assertive, which will lead to greater confidence.

14) Take chances, don't play it safe. If you try to play it safe, your chances of success in life are slim. Be willing to take risks and be open to failure. Even if it fails, you can still make progress. If you're willing to take chances, even if they fail, you will feel proud of yourself. You are giving yourself the potential for success.

15) Don't let others push you. People walking over you will cause you to lose confidence.

16) Adopt high standards. Don't settle for less than you deserve. Accepting whatever you can, subconsciously you are telling yourself that your are a loser.

17) Do not be negative. Negativity negatively affects your mental wellbeing. Negativity can cause you to be angry. You cannot achieve anything if you are negative. If you're constantly negative with your friends, it will lead to them becoming less supportive of you. People that are constantly negative and complaining don't like being around people who complain.

18) Be positive and not negative Being positive makes you happier.

Chapter 10: First Date Tips

Thank you for getting up the courage to ask your beautiful lady out. Now it's the time for your first date. I assume that you're interested in learning more about how to make your first date memorable and so that you can meet again. In dating, it is important to make the right first impression. You have a better chance of landing a second date if your first date goes well. These tips will help you make your first date unforgettable.

Right Place

Usually the guy picks the place. Make sure you pick something that's perfect for your first date. A romantic atmosphere is a good choice. It must be private but not too remote, and it should also be open to the public. A breezy location with lots greenery will add a touch of romance to an afternoon meeting. You may also want to consider setting up a romantic dinner party in a cozy place with soft lighting.

Never be late

Lady should not be forced to wait. Even though this may seem old-fashioned it can help to make an impression. Keep your appointment times. It is better not to wait until she arrives than to be punctual. If you do not pick her up then make sure you reach the venue by the time she arrives. This will ensure that she is relaxed and comfortable upon arrival.

Plan something nice

Plan something nice for your date. Don't let your date know what your date plans are. To ensure that she is prepared, let her know exactly what you're planning. A perfect date usually involves going to more than one place, and must be interesting.

Protective Streak

On their first date, a lot of men forget to show some protection. You don't need to wait until your fifth date before making her feel like royalty. Do your best to make her feel confident and capable of relying on you. Maybe you can make it so that when you cross the street, you are protecting her from other traffic. It is important to remember that small gestures are more valuable than large gestures.

Please Dress Up

It takes time for a woman, especially if she is going on a first date. Remember that first impressions really do count. Dress up to impress and be your best. If she can spend an entire hour getting dressed for a date you can surely do the exact same. Make sure you dress appropriately for the venue. For casual brunches, a dress shirt may not be necessary. If you are planning a special date at an elite restaurant, however, you should wear a dress shirt. Don't be a slob; put some effort into how you look.

The Right Fragrance

You can engage her olfactory and sensual senses when you go out on a date. You will be able to make her feel special by using the right cologne. It will be easy for her to recognize the scent when you're near to her. Avoid strong fragrances, and instead choose fresh or musky scents.

Hygiene Matters

Be a charmer to your date! Take care of your personal hygiene. A well-groomed man is a good thing for everyone. Keep your face and nails trimmed neatly, your nails trimmed and your mouth clean. Bad breath is a big turn off and can even ruin your chances of getting the date. Bring some mints along and make sure to brush your teeth before you meet someone. It's a good idea to get a shower in the morning before the date.

Don't brag

Many men enjoy bragging about their cars and jobs to impress women. Don't be that guy bragging about his job, cars, or other things. Bragging is a big turn off and can make you seem pompous rather that accomplished. If you really want to impress your girlfriend and want her knowledge about your accomplishments than do it subtly. There is a fine distinction between making yourself look great and coming off as arrogant. Pay attention to this. Instead of bragging about you, enjoy this chance to get closer to her. Ask her questions about herself, her work, and, if you are able, discuss your accomplishments. Avoid giving too much detail to her unless she asks. It is important to avoid talking about yourself only.

Never get Drunk

It is easy to get sloppy, especially after having had too many drinks. While it is acceptable to drink, please don't get too drunk. Men sometimes reach for a swig to soothe their nerves when they are feeling anxious or too excited. If you drink too much or become too drunk, this can make it difficult for you to be a good man and distract you from your date. Be careful what you drink. A glass of wine, one or two, or a few of the beverages of your choice is enough. Remember, you are going on a date.

Don't force others to agree with you

You might be certain about the things you want to try or have other ideas. This could be as simple a request to have your date try a particular dish. While it is possible to suggest something, you shouldn't force your partner to try something that she doesn't love. Pushiness is not something anyone enjoys. This can lead to a decrease in chances of you getting another date. If you make your date feel that you are pushing your ideas on her, it will lead to discomfort and she may not be able to have the "perfect" relationship you want.

Get the Hint

You might think you're enjoying your date, but in reality, it might not be. You should also pay attention to what she is saying about herself. Is she happy with the date? Is there anything she finds fascinating or intriguing?

Do you feel distracted or distracted when you first start to talk with your date? Does your date seem to be distracted when you start talking? If you notice any of the above, it is time for you and your partner to switch topics.

It is not necessary that your partner likes all of what you have said. While you may think talking about robotics and cars will make it seem more knowledgeable and interesting than the topic, if your date doesn't like them, it will make everything boring. Be able to read and understand her body language to ensure that the date goes smoothly. You should take her hint when she gives one. But you don't need to be able to talk about only what she likes. It's all fine as long the discussion is fun and entertaining for both of you. Also, try to find common ground so you can both have topics to discuss.

Confidence and trust are important

Confidence is a desirable accessory. This is a positive trait which will make your date feel good. If you don't have the confidence to express yourself, it will show through your body language as well as the way you speak. Your date may quickly notice this. It is clear that you lack confidence and are fighting an uphill battle. It is important to take care of your posture, be straight and confident when speaking. In the following chapters, you'll learn more about how to develop self-confidence.

Keep an eye on yourself

It's easy not to be careful and you might end up with your foot in the mouth. It is better than to be unsafe than sorry. Be mindful of what you are saying, and be cautious. Avoid talking about things that will make her feel uncomfortable. On your first date, avoid discussing politics, expectations from future partners, or any other topics that may make her feel uncomfortable. So how do you decide if a question seems awkward? It is very simple. Ask her nothing you wouldn't want someone asking. You won't want to start a political argument on your first date. If you aren't sure about yourself, you can always make your own list of topics that you can discuss on the first date.

The spirit of chivalry is not dead

You must treat her like a lady. Be kind. You could do as little as helping her into her seat, or opening the door for you. Don't forget to be gentle and respectful. If you are too chivalric and show your chauvinism, you'll come off as a chauvinist. You girls love to be spoilt and doted upon. These are some things you can do to impress your date.

Enjoy a Complimentary Her

People love to be complimented. I am certain that your date loves to be complimented. If used properly, flattery can work wonders. Be careful about what compliments she gives you. Fake compliments are easily detected. To impress her you don't necessarily have to lie. Instead, you can tell her what you admire about them. Do not be afraid to compliment your date about something that you find special or intriguing. Be sure to compliment your date about the clothes she wears. She would have spent many hours choosing her clothes. Making her smile by complimenting her about it is sure to make her smile. You should be careful with the things you say to her.

Chapter 11: Honesty/Vulnerability

Vulnerability means something that an individual's mind will not accept. Vulnerability is a weakness that society today will use to turn against someone who shows it. Even though this is partially true. Vulnerability is not weakness. Being vulnerable means being open to the things you don't like about yourself. Then, be okay with any reactions from others.

Notice that I said they were vulnerable when they accept the opinions of others. They will still care. For a healthy-headed person, they won't. A lot of people attempt to be more confident by not caring much about what others think. When they don't, they beat their heads on the wall. There is no way to be happy about someone else's opinion. Instead, care about their natural human behaviour. You cannot control that.

But you can't control how you react to other peoples' opinions. Let me give an example.

Jim and Greg, there are 2 men. Jim is working hard to build his confidence and self-esteem. To do so, he also tries stop caring about the people around. He believes the only way to attract and feel confident is to treat everyone as if they aren't important. He will then be just like the jerks who he fell in love with. So he does it. But the problem is that every time he's with a girl, he starts to overthink things and to feel guilty. He starts to feel worse about his self and can't even do this one thing. Jim isn't who he pretends to seem in the eyes of others. His brain constantly brings up the truth. He becomes more insecure and needsy every day.

Greg is doing exactly the same thing. However, unlike Jim's, Greg read this book before beginning his confidence journey. He goes out and begins sharing his stories, which he will tell anyone who assumes he is good at something. He will tell them "No, it's actually horrible at that." Greg's ineptness might cause people to reject him. It's OK, those people didn't make Greg happy. Greg now feels a relief he had never felt before.

He feels free. He can finally be himself. It's not his looks or his beach physique. He is now free.

Imagine that you are living your life according to what other people expect you to be. It is like you were holding your true self within a prison cell and finally letting him out. This is how it felt for me. It's like being free from prison. A person that you made for yourself. That's vulnerability. You can stop trying to please everyone and start focusing on what you want.

All that theory talk sounds great. Let's not forget the practical side of things. How to become vulnerable in order to finally be free. As you can see, the title of this chapter is called: "Honesty/Vulnerability". It's because they basically all mean the same things. Being vulnerable means being honest with yourself and sharing a little bit more. This is why I said that the steps in this book all lead to the same thing. Vulnerability is the same thing. Being vulnerable is something you can admit to. It's like giving your throat to strangers. Because it's a risk, people won't do it. Because you show trust and confidence in someone, you can make it attractive for them to trust you. This is how power, long-term, real, honest and happy relationships are made.

For you to be vulnerable, it is important to be truthful. The first and most important thing is to be honest. Telling people what you think about them is important and not expecting anything in return. When we started being friends, I shared my feelings with her and didn't expect her fall in love. I did it just because she seemed like someone trustworthy who can keep my secrets. I also like her for who she is. If she was offended by any one of them, I would know we are not a great fit. However, because we clicked and she loved the real me so we got together. At the time I write this paragraph, it is our first year together.

Some people, but not all of them, won't know how to be truthful. This may sound obvious, but many people will go out telling sad stories about how their mom is cruel and how their dog died. Then they wonder why their little girl didn't go to bed with them. The intention is crucial. It will increase your chances of sleeping with a girl if she asks you instead of listening to you tell her stories and hoping that she will just jump over you.

You must be honest about your intentions. Ask yourself the following question: Do I want to be with her? If the intention is to just sleep with one person, then it can be both. I wouldn't mind meeting with her. You can simply ask if she is interested in spending the night with us. Both you and she will be able to answer the question, which saves time.

If the intention is to meet someone. Tell her stories. Be honest about your experiences, both good and bad. Most importantly, don't make any assumptions about her. If she rejects, great. But if she does not, great. It lets you know if they are really right for you. The truth is that. With the current society, chances of meeting someone trustworthy who loves you for who you really are are very slim. It is almost impossible to meet this person if they lie about your intentions. Because if your lie, you're the problem. If you were to meet every girl you like, and find them cute, you might end-up with the wrong person.

This is why it is so important not to accept a partner. Partner is a lifetime relationship that can make or break your day. To live a happy, fulfilled life, you must choose the right person. Let's not lie and act. We need to be ourselves. We must be sincere, honest, and openly admit that we are wrong. Only then can we find the right person that will love us and appreciate our differences. It's worth it.

I mentioned that vulnerability is not limited to telling the truth. There are many forms and types of vulnerability. The only way to attract a partner is to be vulnerable. Consider it this way: Risking rejection is the only way to show that you want a woman while also showing that your interest in her is less than your own.

Attractiveness requires both investment and desire. Girls must feel they are desired. But, at the same moment, she must be aware that her potential suitor is less invested with her than she is in herself. It's quite paradoxical when you consider it. That's why you have to stick your neck out in front of her so she knows you like her.

However, there are many people who do it and get rejected. Yes, rejection happens. And as you'll see it, it is actually a good sign. Rejections are inevitable and, if they happen, it's likely to be for the best. There are two main reasons why girls get rejected from talking to girls:

#1 Their intentions might not correspond with what is being said

#2 They waited for too long

Let's look at #2 since we just talked about the #1. It's too late for girls to know that you care about them. Girls can sense that your feelings for them are genuine. Insecure people will be unable to express the love they feel for you. This is why you need to be able to express your emotions as quickly as possible.

The number one reason people hesitate to take advantage of opportunities is their lack of self-esteem. We'll discuss ways to fix this problem.

Chapter 12: What Happens When Things Go Wrong

No matter what preparations are made before and during the date. It will not be as perfect as you have planned. It's impossible to make everything go as you wish. It is not always as easy or as straightforward as you think. There are many factors that could cause problems with your date. There are many problems that can occur when everything suddenly turns bad.

There are many reasons you may experience these things. The problem becomes more than a thought. Because you do not understand the circumstances, you ask a lot questions. Am I cursed or lucky? Am I doomed forever to be alone? What are my rights to dating other people? These are just a few other questions to ask yourself when you don't get your date the way that you want.

Even when it seems that all is lost, you can always find a way to save the ship about to sinking that is your relationship. These are two situations that can ruin your evening. And these are ways that you can stop it turning into your worst nightmare.

You made the decision to get sick from all of your days.

Nothing is worse than getting sick before a dinner date. It's very annoying to get sick right before a dinner date you had been looking forward too. When everything is in order but your body won't cooperate. How frustrating can that be? Nobody wants to be the one to impress their date while they cough, snort and wheeze. If you're all sickly and smelly, it is impossible to build romance. That's gross and uncivilized. Here are some ways that you can handle this situation if it does happen to you.

"I got a nasty cold from my brother. Although I was excited about our date, my body is not ready for it. Can we still schedule our date? What about this weekend?

"I do not like to skip my date just because I am having a bad cough. You are welcome to do so. I will be running a little late to rest for awhile.

"I know I am going out on the weekend, but I caught a cold today. I don't like you getting a cold. Let's just schedule for next time.

You decided to make your date look bad.

Murphy's Law. Murphy's Law states, "If there are two or three ways to do something, and one could lead to a catastrophe," then someone will do that. It is because things go from bad-to-worse that this happens. The same goes for dates. There are many different ways a date can turn out and it is possible to screw up. Spilling on someone's clothes is a common mistake.

There are a few people who were born naturally clumsy. Avoid this problem by ordering water. It will save you and your partner from getting into a situation in which one of them ends up cleaning some stains on their clothes. Even though you might be accident-free, you could still have situations similar to this date catastrophe. Here are some ways that you can stop it from becoming worse.

"Ooops. I am so sorry, I spilled some wine onto your (mention where it was). Let me ask for some damp tissue so I can clean it.

"I really meant to not spill some juice onto your (mention where it was). I guess that my clumsy side has shown. My bad. "Let me clean it up."

"I'm sorry, my drink had to go. I'm kidding. Sorry, I spilled some soda water all over your drink (mention the exact location). Thank God it is just water. I'll send some napkins to you so that they can be dried.

"I didn't mean to spill some Coca-Cola on your (mention the place where you drank it). Let's make sure you use the bathroom. "I am really sorry."

There is an emergency.

Your date can be disrupted in several situations. An emergency is one such. You may need to respond immediately to a family or work emergency. Emergencies can happen unexpectedly and are not planned. But some people make it appear one to avoid ending a very boring relationship. This is rude and your date should not be treated this way. Make sure you only use the "emergency" card if it is necessary. Karma has a way to get back to you.

If your phone rings at odd times and someone calls you, be polite to your date. You are just being polite and your date will appreciate your apology. You should take your time explaining the situation to your date, even if it is an emergency. Don't rush. You could be accused of making assumptions about your "emergency". You don't have to be rude when you break the news about your date.

"I really regret, but we can cut the date. There is an urgent situation at the house. My mom suffered a severe heart attack. If I have to go to the hospital for a heart attack, would you mind driving me there?

"Would there be a way to bring you with me to the office to check on something?" My boss called and said that it was an emergency. I don't wish to leave you. It will take a while, but it won't be hard. We will be able to grab dinner later, I promise."

"My sister was in an automobile accident. "I'm sorry, but I need you to take her to the hospital. I don't want to drag your evening so I can bring you home. You can even come with me to hospital if you are not comfortable asking.

"I didn't anticipate this, but there is a house emergency. Do you mind rescheduling our date? I will call you tomorrow. I am truly sorry for this."

Where is your wallet?

It's not something people do every day. It's usually after the meal that you check for it. After dinner, it is time to check your wallet.

You check your coat, you check your pocket. It isn't there. It turns out, you forgot your money because you were too anxious about the date. You now have to make the payment for your date's dinner.

These situations can endanger your future prospects. This can lead to a loss of future opportunities. Now, neither of you should take it personally on the person who took the wallet. For a fun way to end the night, laugh it off.

"It's fine (mention his/her names). I have the next one. "Would you like to get the next?

"Don't worry (mention him or her name). It's not that big of a deal, I also forgot my wallet. I'll accept the check and pay for the next.

Chapter 13: Confidence, It's Vital

If this book inspires me in any way, it's the realization of how crucial your confidence is for this process. You can't love yourself if you don't have confidence. It's almost impossible for someone to love you or like you if you don't love yourself.

Confident men attract women. These are tips to boost your self-confidence if it isn't enough.

#1 - Self-affirmation through positive self-talk

This book says more than that you just need to be happier. This book teaches you how to keep your positive energy focused on yourself. Consistently practicing self-affirmations is a great way to achieve this goal. While you can make self-affirmations prior to the date of your wedding, it is much better to keep them going. Anything you can think of yourself that inspires positivity in you is a self affirmation. You have the option of looking in the mirror and repeating self-affirmations over and over, while simultaneously looking at your own reflection. Or, if you prefer, you can sit down to write down all your self affirmations. Both are great.

Tell yourself why and how you love it. Tell yourself you're the best man. Remind yourself of the incredible things that you've done. Be confident that you can accomplish whatever you put your mind too. Confidence is a virtue.

A positive mindset is a way to be more confident.

#2 - Lift weights

For self-confidence, lifting weights and exercising can be powerful tools. Your confidence will increase if you do any exercise. It's sometimes difficult to see your mental progress towards becoming more positive. It can be seen physically by working out and exercising.

Your running times will improve if you run a half-mile every day. You'll notice an increase in stamina and endurance when you exercise. Lifting weights is a great way to change your body.

Nothing can be more motivating then seeing positive changes within yourself. These changes will help you be more confident.

#3 – Do something that you are very good at

We are all good at one thing. It doesn't really matter what skill you have. Doing more of it will make it more enjoyable.

Do you have the ability to defeat others in a specific game? Try it. Are you a great basketball player? Do some basketball. Are you an expert at organizing and cleaning up your room? Make sure you clean and organize your room.

It's possible that you're struggling at just a few areas of your life, which can lead to a lack of confidence. Instead of dwelling on the things you can't accomplish, think about what you can. Concentrate on the things you are truly good at and that will bring confidence to other aspects of your daily life.

#4 – Live by your principles

Are you guided by principles? Are you living your life according to your mission statement? If not, it's time for you to develop some principles and incorporate them into your life mission. As a CEO would write a business statement, you will decide which principles are most important to your life. You are crafting a vision that you can stand by.

After you have set some principles, follow them. Be true to them. Your confidence will grow if you are able to live up to your rules. It doesn't matter if you write your principles down or type them up on your computer.

If you live by the principles that you believe, you create small successes each day by sticking to what you believe.

#5- Change your body language

Sometimes all it takes for confidence to be boosted is to alter your body language. This can be done by changing your posture, standing, or making small, permanent changes.

Stand straight up and keep your posture good. Be taller more often. When you're speaking to someone, be more relaxed. If you change your body language, it will not only make you more confident but also help you appear more confident.

#6 – Set a small but achievable goal and strive to reach it

It is common for us to set unrealistic goals that we don't have the means to achieve in the time and space that we desire. Consider setting smaller goals you know you can achieve. Each goal should be small and achievable. It doesn't matter how small or large the goal. Setting an objective and reaching it will build confidence as you know you're doing what you said.

Consider setting a goal to clean your room. It should be easily achievable, and you will feel fantastic afterward. It doesn't matter if you have to grocery shop. You should set that goal. It doesn't matter if you are trying to get 3 miles per day. Set the goal to exercise at any level. You'll be able to exercise regardless of whether you run a half-mile, walk around the block, and do ten pushups.

These are the small things that make us feel good about ourselves. Self-confidence can be built by feeling better about yourself.

#7 – Stop comparing oneself to another

People in today's social world compare themselves with others at a higher frequency than ever before. Many people begin to compare their lives to others. It may happen subconsciously without your realizing.

Be mindful that you are only seeing the best bits of others' lives. These posts, texts and images will only show you what they want. If you see only what you want to see in others, you can be apathetic about your own life and self-worth.

Remember that you are always going be exactly who and what you are.

Pre-date confidence boosts

Sometimes, a date approaching can make us anxious. It happens to everyone. It's natural. You shouldn't let this nervousness turn into anxiety.

There are proven techniques that can help boost confidence, even for a fraction.

Sometimes you just need a little boost in your confidence to get yourself out of a panicky or worried mood. Here are a few things that can give you confidence before your date.

#1 – The self-pep talk.

Sometimes you just need a little encouragement. Look in the mirror. Do you feel proud of yourself? Tell yourself that you are the best man. Tell yourself you value your principles and values and will stand by them.

Tell yourself that the woman whom you are about to meet likes you. Tell yourself how confident your are.

Be sure to look at yourself in each sentence. "You got this! You're the man You hold true to your values and principles She likes you! She loves my confidence."

#2 - Self-affirmation loop

What is the difference? Focus. You can get distracted by your thoughts when searching your brain to find affirmations for yourself. You might feel negative emotions or be distracted which can cause you to lose focus on the positive.

Take a look at all the affirmations about yourself, and then choose the three most positive affirmations. Keep repeating these three affirmations in a loop. This loop will keep you on track, and help you boost your confidence.

#3 - A hero stance

This has been tried and proven to be effective by social scientists. It has been used by millions worldwide, so it doesn't matter if you've ever heard of it. The idea is that posing as a superhero for two minutes will increase your testosterone, or dominance, level by approximately 20% and decrease your cortisol, or stress hormone, level by about 25%.

The superhero pose, which I affectionately call the "hero" stance, is when you are tall with your chest out and your shoulders back. You also have your hands in your fists, just below your waist. With your chin up, you look forward and pretend to be a hero. This will help reduce stress.

According to these statistics testosterone levels, stress levels, and self-confidence are directly related, you can improve your self esteem by 45% by pretending like a hero for two minutes before your date.

You can't fake self-confidence

Most women can smell confidence when it is faked by men. You can't fake self-confidence; you must have it. Self-confidence means trusting and believing in your abilities, talents, and judgment. Knowing what you're capable of. Knowing what you are skilled at. It is important to believe that the conclusions and reasoning you make about situations are reasonable and logical. Don't fake it. Follow the tips and be confident!

Chapter 14: Remember What You Text Your Girl

"It's pointless to be exact when you don't know what you're talking about."

The new standard of communication is texting. It is the preferred method of communication for Generation Z, Millennials, and Generation Z to communicate their thoughts. Sometimes, texting works better than face-to-face conversations. Because some things are too embarrassing, or inappropriate, some people find text messages more useful for communicating their thoughts and feelings.

Shy people are especially fond of text messages. They don't have to speak with others anymore. Anything significant can be communicated through texts, without the additional pressure of having others react.

Texting is also much more relaxing. If you have nothing to contribute to the conversation, you don't need to worry so much about texting. Even in the first stages of courtship, when you start to get to know each others better, there will be times when you don't know what you should say. You quickly scan your surroundings for something of interest and then rush to make a decision.

You may find texting useful because it doesn't require you to answer immediately. Texting is a way to be patient and take your time. It allows you to answer only when you are certain that the message is accurate.

However, texting can be easy but it is still important to talk to girls and keep them interested. Texting can be an effective tool, and it can do wonders for your career if you understand how to use it.

This chapter will help clarify the mistake you made and give you some tips to improve your texting skills.

Keep Her Interest

Texting skills are a major problem for men because they don't take it seriously.

The world is changing. How we express emotions and thoughts is changing. Maintaining interest in a woman can be difficult when you have no skills and there are other men waiting for you to jump at.

After you meet her, text her immediately

This is essential. Don't wait until you have spoken to the girl or exchange numbers before you text her. It's best to text your first message within twenty-four hour of meeting the girl. An example message would be "Hey James," which could indicate your interest and desire to communicate with her.

These messages, such as "Hey (hername), James from last Thursday's dinner party," are not considered rude or inappropriate. However, the delay you showed could indicate that you weren't aware she was interested in you for a while. This could be detrimental to you.

Begin an Interesting Conversation for You

You can't count on her to lead the charge. Most likely, she won't. You have already sent her a message, so you decide how to continue your conversation. The more attractive and open you are to her, the more you will get to know each other.

It is easy to text a girl saying "what's going on?" and get a reply that says "nothing, you?". This makes it hard to start a new conversation, as it becomes boring. Your first impression can be the most important.

How do you want your first message from her to unfold? It all comes down to your preference. This text could serve as a starting point for a conversation.

"Would that make you happier? Unlimited money or superpower?". You can also text her to ask, "What are the top modern trends that you find annoying?"

These texts will prompt her to think. This will create a lively conversation. You'll also get to know each others better by sharing your answers. This will help spark your potential romance.

Do Not Let It Get Stale

You've succeeded in getting her attention. Now, it's time to bring new ideas to the conversation and keep it from becoming boring.

It doesn't matter how dynamic you are with the girl, there are many ways that you can do it. Discover new topics of interest, which could include current affairs or discussing your favourite movies. Take the time to get to know your girl and never stop the excitement.

Let her Know That You Think of Her

For her to grasp the meaning of your words, you don't necessarily have to speak directly. You could let her know by subtle signals that you care about and support her. Texts wishing you a good day and goodnight are very appealing to women. Send her original, not rewritten messages.

You send her good morning or goodnight texts, which means that you are thinking of her first thing after getting up in the morning and then your last thing before falling asleep. This is an excellent example of a original text: "Best wishes for your interview today. You will succeed." She shouldn't be sent "good morning". It is impersonal.

Text Back Quickly

The speed with which you reply to her texts is what girls first notice. If you respond to her quickly, she will notice that you are interested. She will make every effort to get in touch with you. The conversation will flow.

If she texts you to tell you that she's going to the store to get groceries, her reply will be incongruous and unneeded. You should not respond because the moment is gone.

There are many ways to get her to text you.

Now that you have gained her attention and all is well, it is the time to make your moves. You don't have the need to be upfront about it at first but ensure that she feels you are interested.

Use Her Name in Your Texts

The most beautiful thing is when people use their names in their messages. This applies to all genders, not just women. This signifies that the conversation was personal and not merely generic. That was the only text that you sent to her. It wasn't something that you copied and pasted to other women.

Do not immediately begin using pet names. This will cause her to think you are too forthright, which is a major turnoff for most women.

Texts like "hello, sweetheart/darling/baby/honey" are not only highly forward and personal but, when used early on, look like you are trying too hard, not to mention cringe-worthy and corny.

Proper grammar is essential for spellings and grammar.

A man who uses proper grammar and spelling is loved by women because it shows maturity and intelligence. Bad grammar, incorrect spellings and other errors can make it difficult to get a deal. Immature abbreviations of words and shortening of them are also immature. It makes you look like you are still high school.

Texts that say "hey ho" or use of "y" as an alternative to "why," "2", rather than too/to", or "r", instead of "are" are also not attractive. It is best not to text a girl saying "can't we8 2 c U 2nite" and hoping she will keep interest in you.

Some abbreviations might be fine, such "np", for "no problems" or "yk," for "you knew," but it's best to not go too far. Don't be a teenager texting his first time.

Flirting or playful teasing

It may not work out for you if your character is boring and nice. You must add spice to your texts to keep the spark alive. This could include flirting and playful teasing. Don't respond to her messages only with simple responses. Give it a personality boost and flirt with your client to keep her on the edge of her seat.

Text messages with phrases like "you're such an idiot" or laughing at her liking cheesy romantic rom-coms are a fun way for her to retain the spark and make you laugh.

Emojis and the Art of Emojis

You may be familiar now with texting techniques, but I haven't discussed an essential aspect to texting. Emojis. Because they don't know how or when to use them, Emojis are a bane on many men's existence.

You need to be careful when and how you use certain emojis. Otherwise, they could send the wrong message which can get you in trouble and endanger your budding romance.

Emojis were developed from Japanese culture. Much meaning gets lost in translation. These people keep creating meanings for the emojis which are not universal. Most people can't even understand them.

Emojis' Implied Meaning

Another problem is that emojis have an implied meaning. Many emojis may have an incorrect meaning in the texting world, making it difficult to use them literally. The eggplant emoji is not appropriate for talking about your grandma's famous recipe. Or the splashing emoji for ocean lovers.

Similar, cherry and peach emojis as well as hotdog, hotdog, or taco emojis can't be used to replace their food equivalents.

Remind yourself that smiling faces emojis during argument are a terrible idea. It is the emoji equivalent if "no offense" to something that is always offensive.

Proper Emoji Use

Knowledge of emojis can help avoid any confusion. If you are not certain of the meaning, don't use an emoticon. Consider carefully what certain emojis mean before you use them.

Don't cry laughing when she loses her dog. She may think that it is a sign of sadness and that you are supporting her. You are laughing at the woman for being upset about her dead dog.

Emojis can be prone to misinterpretation. Your girl may not know of an emoji or see it differently. Perhaps she is an Android user. Your Apple smile might look more like a grin.

Emojis should be used sparingly. Emojis from men are often too explicit for girls. Use your words and emotions to convey your emotions.

Texting is an art that is easily learned. This will help you to get to understand your girl better.

Chapter 15: One Night Stands

If you are looking for a "One Night Stand", there are a few things you can do to improve your chances. First, it is important to find a dating platform or app that allows you messaging women. Once you have chosen the right dating site or app for you, you should send as many "first" messages as you can. You may or not need to lower the standards, depending on how thirsty your are for a single night. You also have to adjust your age, travel distance and eliminate any filters.

Once that's done, you can start messaging women you are attracted too. If you want your chances to be more successful, message women one to two points lower up on the attractiveness score. For example, if your usual dating habits are to date women who are 8's or higher, you might consider lowering that number to 7's or 6's. You will have more options. I have had the pleasure of meeting a few women that were not as attractive on their profiles but who turned out to be hot in person. I learned from these experiences that not all women look photogenic. Some women may look hot in photos, but not always in person. This is why it's important to remember this when looking at profiles. I have often met women and dated them the same day as they first met me on the dating app or site. I believe that Saturdays work best. Here's my reasoning: If her friends are out with their partners or husbands, but she's home alone on Saturday night, then she'll feel lonely.

Now she's looking through social media to see her friends' pictures of their evenings and decides to log onto her online dating account to search for a man she can meet up for drinks. Most women looking to meet someone will not say that they would like to have sex. Some women will only tell you by text. Some prefer to meet up face-to-face to feel your vibe. Never give her your address without first meeting you in person. Always pick the meeting place (preferably in close proximity to your place). If she chooses the location, make sure that you use Google Maps to explore the area. Do not force any woman to meet you! Remember, NO! means NO! No! You have to be socially aware and have the ability to recognize when she is uncomfortable. Men can become aroused quickly and be turned on instantly. It's like flipping a light switch to turn it on. Women work better as volume knobs. For a louder sound, increase it gradually.

You have unlimited access to women across the globe when you use online dating. I will make sure to update my profile with the new location before I travel. To avoid any potential misunderstandings, always have at least two backups. This is a great option to have someone with you while on your travels. Most often, they will pick you up at your airport and drive to your hotel. It was possible that we would have sex in our hotel rooms as soon as we arrived. It's possible to sex with more women than you meet on dating apps and sites during your stay.

It is important to note that some women may not be comfortable sharing their number with you if they're just looking for a quick date. They prefer to communicate with you via dating sites, email, and google voice. I had one night with a 48-year old wealthy woman. She contacted me only via email. I respect that decision. Respect the form of communication she chooses to use. Below is a screenshot I took of the email she sent. After our intimate evening at The Plaza Hotel NYC in NYC, she sent us this email. The Plaza is an extremely luxurious hotel, located close to Central Park. Now she suggested we meet there. We decided to book a place there for a couple of drinks. She paid for it, but I paid for the drinks. It was an unforgettable evening. That was the only time I had had sex with her. I was too busy with other ladies. Although she did try to reach me, it was not possible to commit to anything due to my hectic schedule.

Men are looking for something serious

Don't give up on your search for something serious, men! There are many women online who are interested in the same things you are. No matter whether you're looking for long term relationships, a committed marriage, or just casual dating. You will need to be willing and able to go through the weeding process. Sometimes you may have to go to 5, 10, 15, or 20 dates before you can find a potential partner. However, it is also possible that you go on less than five dates and meet her. Be patient, keep positive, and don't rush to find the right woman for you. Don't be too rigid in trying to find a match for you on every aspect of life. That's just impossible. Instead, try to focus on the genuine relationship and commonalities you have with one another. The rest can be built upon. Your profile should be truthful. You want her (or anyone else) to feel attracted to the real you. On your "About Me", you might add more detail about your interests, hobbies and goals. You can keep your bio brief but include all relevant information in all categories. Plenty of Fish (POF), carried out a study which examined word choice in dating profiles. Researchers observed that those who used "love," more often, were more successful in finding it. Additionally, they discovered that men would benefit from the words, "heart," children, romance, and "relationship."

There were many women that I met online who I felt I could trust and I did not want to sleep with. I was not looking forward to being "the man" they wanted to have sex. I've been there. It's nothing but headaches. If you don't mind leading women along, it's okay. But I don't have the time for games and I try to keep my words as truthful as possible. I made friends with a few of the women, and we still maintain contact for business purposes.

The paid dating sites or apps you use are often the best at finding high quality women. This is not true. While there are many quality women on these dating sites and apps, you must also go through the weeding process. There are many different types of women online, including those who are looking for short or long-term relationship, marriage, or non-monogamous relationships. Also, there are women who will try to rob and rob you. Do not let them rob your life! Be mindful of these types of women. They'll ask you for your permission to meet them in strange places. I prefer to pick the meeting spot. If she isn't happy with my choice, we will both choose a different place.

I have heard many stories of men getting robbed when the woman they were meeting said he should meet her at "123 Main ST" by a dark alley behind a building. There, a group, or should that be punks, are waiting to rob you. When I hear stories such as this, I think, "What the heck could these men do to get robbed like this?" Then I ask myself my own question. "Honrny fucking guys thinking with their penis!". But I've heard many stories of people finding love online, marrying, continuing to be married, starting families, and keeping a loving, healthy marriage. Please men, stay positive. You will reach the end goal. I believe in you and know that you will. Even if the book isn't for you, you can still benefit from the advice and lessons.

Chapter 16: How to Instantly Improve and Improve Your Game

It is possible to believe that not all theories regarding the dating industry are true. Some of these theories are based in scientific evidence and years worth of research conducted by university professors. These theories will help you improve your game and find a girlfriend.

One example is the beer goggles thesis. This theory suggests women choose men based purely on their time. The theory was supported by scientific research. The research found that women tend to be more picky at the end of the day than they are at the beginning of the day. Because most women want to get together in the early hours of morning, this is why they tend to be more open to dating. Thus, chances of you meeting someone are higher if you start looking at girls during the night.

A theory exists that women dress according ovulation. Most women will show more skin if they have ovulating or are available. Your chances of finding the right women for you are higher if your search is based on the way they dress. You will also be able connect with more women.

Another thing to understand about women is the similarity factor. This factor is based upon how many things you have to do with the women you are dating. This means that if you have similar tastes in food or enjoy going to the parks together, you will be more likely to get along with her and become her boyfriend. Choose a girl who is interested in your music and style if you want to be with a woman for a long time.

The true key is changing yourself

It is important to remember that the most important thing right now is changing your mindset. It is essential that you have the right attitude and the right moves to get a girlfriend. Your chances of having a girlfriend are low if the majority of your life is spent in the house playing computer games and not out doing anything. If you are looking to get the girl in your dreams, it is time to start changing your lifestyle.

Your look is the most important thing. Changes in your appearance require you to learn how to look better, be more hygienic and to make your body look better. You must learn to take a better bath and to trim your nose hair. If you have long or bushy hair, you must learn how to trim your hair properly so you don't look like a hippie. You should also learn how to apply cosmetic products to remove pimples and blackheads.

Your clothing should be updated. Instead of wearing a plain shirt, learn how you can wear formal wear. Wear a nice polo and a formal tie with a blazer. Black leather shoes or other formal footwear is also a must. It doesn't matter if your clothing makes you look better. You do not need to dress up or wear fancy accessories, as peacocking seems like a myth.

However, to look great you have to feel great. It is essential to exercise regularly if you want to feel great. A man who regularly goes to the gym and loves sports is sure to be a suitable boyfriend. In order to attract women, you should exercise regularly. Exercise as often and eat well. Reduce your intake of alcohol and quit smoking to improve your overall health and appearance.

Finally, learn how women communicate. With constant practice, learn how to speak slowly and in depth. This is done by looking in the mirror. Then, speak calmly and with courage to yourself. Check out some cool jokes and read about other topics that interest women. As long as your ability to make a woman giggle and make her feel special, you will always have her attention. Once you have gained her trust, start to date her. You will soon be her girlfriend.

The best way to find a girlfriend is to meet as many women. Ask women that you pass in bars, restaurants and discos. The more women you meet the easier it is to have conversations with women. You only need to be there for each other and not be too picky. Meet new people. Even if a girl doesn't want to be paired with you, it is not a sign of weakness. Get to know the girls and make new friends.

Chapter 17: Keeping It Strong

Finding the right partner is just one step. One of the most important steps in a relationship is keeping it going. What is the third? How to identify if the relationship you are in is healthy. Perhaps you have had several bad relationships. Now you are wondering what a healthy and happy relationship looks like. If this is the case, you're not the first person to wonder. Even couples that have been married for some time might not know if the relationship they are in is healthy. It is true that their partner is happy. But, does this make them healthy?

What a healthy relationship should look like

You might have different ideas about what normal or healthy relationships look and feel like. A healthy, normal relationship might look different if it was shaped by family members who were constantly at odds or involved in harmful behaviors. It could be that you have an understanding of healthy relationships because you grew up with family members who supported and loved one another.

It's a fact that relationships are always evolving and changing. As the couple grows together, learns, and adapts, so does their relationship. As these changes take place, some couples find themselves closer to one another and are more sensitive towards the needs of their partner. Some couples end up drifting apart and falling apart after they're unable to weather the storms together. It was because their relationship exhibited the essential characteristics of a healthy relationship, which gave them the strength to endure the challenges and prevail.

What does it look like to have a healthy partnership? If your relationship displays these characteristics, you'll have lots of reasons to smile. Your relationship with the man you love is healthy and full promise for the foreseeable future.

Trust again. Trust. Trust is an absolute and crucial element of a relationship that can give it a fighting chance. It is the foundation of any successful relationship. Without this, it's difficult to build all the elements necessary for a lasting relationship. Trust is an essential element of a healthy relationship. It's that easy.

Your partner has made you better. You not only make each other more beautiful, but your relationship can also help you be better. You are able to bring out the best and be more for your man.

There's no reason to be afraid of your man. If your relationship with your man is healthy, however, you might not be capable of making all your troubles disappear. But being around him can ease your fears. He makes you feel loved and supported. You don't feel scared or worried as much when you're by yourself.

A Healthy Dose Communication - Couples who communicate well together stay together. A healthy relationship requires that both partners communicate respectfully, honestly, and feel comfortable enough with their partner to discuss anything. Healthy couples can talk about it, and they can then address each other's concerns. Finally, they can work together as a group to find a solution. They don't pretend that everything is perfect, and they won't allow problems to get in the way of their happiness. They make it a point of talking about it.

Patience: A healthy relationship is one that has patience, understanding, love and compassion. While it may not be possible to always be patient, couples in healthy relationships make every effort and practice patience. If one person is having an awful day, the other person tries their best to be patient and supportive until the other feels better. Both partners will attempt to accept the moods of the other when they feel down.

A lot of Empathy – The ability to empathize, understand and view your partner's perspective can make a significant difference in your relationship dynamics. Empathy can transform how you handle conflicts and deal with them. This is just as important as trust and is crucial for a healthy relationship.

There is still Chemistry between you. Although your relationship may be less intense than it was when they first met, there is still good chemistry. Even years later, the two of you can still have a happy and healthy relationship. The strong connection you have allows your feelings of lust and love to grow, and it keeps the chemistry between you going.

You are both invested – When both partners feel invested, they will be more likely to put in extra effort -- especially in addressing issues they aren't happy with. A healthy relationship dynamics is one in which both partners are open to finding the best solution for their partner and they are also committed to staying positive.

You Can See The Difference From the Past - When you can clearly see the differences between what you have now and what you had previously, it is an indicator that you are now in a healthy partnership. There's always a reason that those relationships didn't work out. If your current relationship is significantly better, happier and more successful, you'll know you're on the right path.

Willingness and ability to be flexible - To make relationships work, there must be compromise. It is essential that both partners are flexible. Otherwise it will be difficult to maintain a healthy relationship.

There's Ample Gratitude - Research shows that appreciation and gratitude are the keys to happiness and lasting relationships. It is important to feel appreciated in your relationship. This will help improve the overall wellbeing of your relationship. Both partners feel more content when they are able to express their appreciation for eachother, even for the small things they do.

If you and your partner are planning for the future together, this is one of the most important indicators that you have a healthy relationship. You can tell that your partners have similar goals and visions. This is a sign they are planning to move forward together.

Dynamics of a Healthy Marriage

Happy Couples have the following habits

Happy couples don't work hard together. They have routines and habits that help them stay happy. Here are some happy couples' common habits that keep their smiles on each other's faces.

They Have a Common Ritual – Happy couples will make it a habit to share one or several rituals. It could involve sharing the chores of brushing teeth together, cooking together, and even helping with the dishes.

Going to Bed Together- Happy couples have a shared habit of going together to bed. It was exciting to be able to get out of bed at the same hour when you first started a relationship. The comfort of falling asleep alongside your partner is wonderful, and happy couples have made it their goal to keep this tradition alive as much as possible.

Always be kind with compliments. Happy couples don't stop complimenting one other. It keeps the love alive.

They Create Shared Interests. Happy couples will find common interests. They cultivated shared interests they didn't have before.

Hug eachother - Make it a habit to hug for at least ten minutes every day. You could do it before you go back to bed at night, in the morning, while you're getting up, or anytime you feel like a hug. A warm hug from someone you love is one the most comforting feelings.

They Hold Hands. - If they'ren't holding hands but are walking side by side, it's at least that they're still in the same place. This is how happy partners enjoy each other. They remain close to each other even when they're away.

They kiss before they leave - When one of their partners is about to go, happy couples make it an habit to kiss goodbye to remind the other to have a good day and that you love them.

They Make Forgiveness And Trust a Priority. If forgiveness and trust are two of the most important things in a happy couple's lives, it is making them a priority. They are quick to forgive one another when they disagree. They trust one another to be their support system. They also trust their partners enough not to feel uneasy or suspicious when their partner is around other people.

They Are More Focused on the Good Things. While every relationship will have its ups and downs, happy couples always focus more on what is good. They know that the worst times will never come back and they should not waste any time. The good times are what they cherish the most because they make every moment of being together worth it.

They don't nag, nitpick or nag - Happy couples try to avoid unnecessarily nagging and nitpicking at each other. They know that this does not warm someone's heart so instead they do the right thing and talk about it.

They Say "I Love You Everyday" - Tell someone that you love them every day, as you never know when it might be your last. Happy couples do this every day to remind each other that they are loved. To set the mood for a happy day, hugging your partner is a wonderful way to tell them you love and support them. When you receive a message that you are loved, you will feel happy.

They Wish Each Other A Great Day - Everyday brings its challenges. However, happy couples set a positive tone to help their partner start the day. To make your partner's day better, all they have to do is wish them a great day.

Good Morning, Good Night - Good morning to each other when they wake and good night when they go back to sleep. Even if they have an argument, no matter how bitter they are, happy couples who make it a point not to say sorry to their partner send the message that the love they share is still important, no matter what.

They create their own joy - When life gets a little monotonous and boring, happy couples make it their business to break away from the norm. Happy couples share a genuine love for each other, which is one of the reasons their relationship flourishes even when many others are falling apart. When they feel the need, they are open to trying new things and creating their own fun bond.

Check in With Them: Happy couples will check in together throughout the day to see how each other is doing. If their partner is having an awful day, they try to cheer him up. If their partner is having an amazing day, they can share the joy. It's these little gestures that remind each other how much their care.

They are proud to be with their partners - Happy couple are proud to be together. They are not ashamed, embarrassed, or in competition with other strangers to find the best-looking partner. They're happy when they are with someone they love and it's all they care about.

No Phone Policy. - This is possibly the most important, most effective and powerful habit that couples can have to keep their relationship happy. They are present with their partner and make it a point not to text or call each other when they're together. After the quality bonding is complete, all other activities such as browsing social media updates and responding to messages can be put on hold. It is becoming a very common sight to see couples at dinner and instead of having a conversation, scrolling through phones and enjoying the company of their friends.

A happy relationship is only possible if you put in the effort. A happy relationship is one that two people work together.

Chapter 18: How to face the call to agreement on the date

How do I get her to feel that special bond that you had in your previous meeting with me?

Simple!

If she was keen to participate in one or more activities, you will be able to call her. Simply say hello with the nickname you invented, or quote Hawaii (referring specifically to the first example), to instantly recall what you felt at the moment of complicity.

As you can see, it doesn't take much to make yourself nice enough to go on a date. Complicity and Passions can be done in advance so you are ready for the journey (downhill) to meet her.

If you are just starting out in seduction or have a burning desire to have some sex, it is possible to fall into the trap. Chatting with her may become boring and heavy. She might have other things to do.

Also, you can't kiss her on the phone and have sex.

Don't make the mistake to make several long phone calls. She may continue to postpone your date.

The phone call should make her want to do something with YOU, just like she did the first time she saw you. (See previous chapters). You'll then need to make the same speech for the XXX Course, the YYY Store, and the ZZZ Lesson to give her additional information.

Prepare to be amazed as I reveal the secret behind how I transformed so many real NOS into real dates.

My mistake, like many others, wasn't in the destination or the place where I was to meet but rather in how I wrote the request.

To ask the girl for permission to go out, my conditional and uncertain tone were used. This was interpreted by her as a pleading.

It was basically like this:

What could a girl make of such a request for her? It is not interesting.

It is essential to tease and intrigue your partner when you plan to meet up for a date.

Make a firm statement. Pretend that she wants to go on a date with you. How to make it happen? These examples will be very helpful for you:

*"... I made sure that the XYZ Course Instructor would accept you at Tuesday's

lesson. See you there around 9 PM, or pick you up a little sooner."

* "... * "... Are we going to there at 11.30 or 16,?

*"... the friend that I was telling of said that there is a special occasion all week. "I'm very busy on Tuesday. What can we do on Monday and Wednesday?"

*" ... *"... You'll find me there around 18:45. I suggest you get out of work a little earlier so you don't miss anything!

*"... On Tuesday and Thursday, we train at Volleyball.

*"... I managed to get a pass in the trial lesson. Although the course has started a few months ago, we found ourselves there a little later so I will give you a quick overview. Let's meet Wednesday morning at 21.30 in front XYZ square, all dressed in red.

Note the end

You don't need to wait for her conversation to turn dull and monotonous to open the call. Call her at a time she is highly emotional (a laugh), a particular affectionate or malicious tone, curiosity and desire to chat

I will offer some practical suggestions that are based upon my own experience. These tips may not be universal but most times they work.

*Be sure to always pick the day, date, and time. She will always tell you if it is not right. Not to be flexible but to show that your ideas are clear and you know what you are doing. Don't be afraid if you have to make changes to your programs. He may be testing you. Men who favour women too much aren't liked by them. For example, if she tells you that she can't do it on Tuesday, then let's do it Wednesday

at 19." You shouldn't tell them "ok okay", retract some points and have the last say. Then tell her instead that "Wednesday is a study day with others until late. Okay for me, but we do it at 7.30 pm close to the library."

*Most people prefer to have dates during the first week. This is because they will not be busy on Fridays or Saturdays with their friends.

*You can choose to go on an afternoon rather than an evening date if you are free. This will help her feel more at home and safer.

*Do not spend too much time or too little between your first and second meetings to call her. You might appear too involved if your first call is on the same day. If you give her too much time, she may feel you don't care enough or call you for makeshift. Two to three days is usually fine.

*Don't call your girlfriend today to ask her to go out tonight. Women need to get organized.

Chapter 19: The Creep Factor and How To Avoid Being Misunderstood.

Webster's Online Dictionary defines the term "crawl" to mean "an unpleasant or obnoxious human being."

The way you approach women while you're on your online dating journey will decide whether you come off as a creep or genuine man who is worth dating.

Your online approach to women will influence the adjectives or nouns they use about you. This is why it is important to not come off as a creep when dating.

Recap: You can avoid being called creepy by optimizing and updating your online dating profile. This includes your bio, pictures, and bio. Next, follow the tips for sending the first message. Use messaging in a way which builds rapport and flirtation and drives the interaction towards a date or pre-date.

If you adhere to this advice, there should be no reason to worry. When you communicate with the women that you meet online, it will be from a position of genuine curiosity and a desire to learn more about them. That is how authentic men come across.

This chapter adds to the information you already have on how to initiate genuine online interactions.

How to Avoid Being Labeled "Creepy"

Here are some tips to help you avoid being labelled a creep.

#: Keep the PG13 version.

As we were discussing ways to make an online dating profile that is attractive, we agreed on one strategy: avoid taking inappropriate photos of yourself in the bathroom or showing your naked body. Follow this advice and it should be extended to all areas of your interactions.

It's important that you keep the PG13 status of your messages to her confidential. She should not receive "dick pictures" and any other unsolicited images. You should only use funny memes/GIFs.

Now we will be talking about keeping it under PG13.

#: Avoid sex talking

You should not mention sex during your first ten interactions with a woman whom you've just met online. Yes, you think sex should be important. As with physical-based compliments - the next strategy - mentions sex in your initial interactions sets off alarms for her mind. She will then think you are a sexual pervert looking to find an "easy laid."

In addition, this book indicates that you are searching for a girlfriend (or long-term companion) and are currently reading it. It is possible that you will receive unsolicited sex offer from men every day if you mention that you want a beautiful, high quality woman. Mentioning sexuality will cause her to bundle you up with the men she is trying to ignore, block, or filter out.

#: Do not forget physical-based compliments

It's important that this point is not only mentioned in another section, but it is also worth repeating.

Only compliment her body when you are building attraction or flirtation.

#: Serial SMS

It's easy for a match to be overdone if you start to text her frequently, especially if she doesn't respond quickly or takes too long to reply.

Serial-texting has become a popular mistake. Your match will not be interested in your messages and will make an accusation of you as an online dating creep.

Remember, the high-quality woman that you want to attract will be busy living her own life and "getting hers". By being gentle, you can respect her and show restraint.

Sending her more than one message at a time is not a good idea. You need to wait for a response before you send another. Sending text-for -text is the best way to communicate with her. Send your message to her after she replies. Do not send a follow-up message if she does not reply in a few days.

#: Over-forwardness

It is possible to have a romantic relationship with her. However, it will not only help you build rapport and attraction.

In a world in which women are used hearing things like "hey cutie," "hottie," "babe", etc., or statements such as, "you have the bangin' body," flirting too fast, especially with strangers, will get her creep-radar and make you unmatched.

It is important to remember that women can judge you by what you speak. Be open to talking to her and showing her you can be the perfect partner.

If you do this and are authentic and genuine in your desire to establish a connection with the woman that you match with, then you shouldn't have any problems with getting away with the creep tag.

Avoid costly dating-profile mistakes to ensure that women who meet you on dating sites do not misunderstand your character or call you creepy.

Let us briefly discuss how to avoid making such errors.

Avoid these Dating Profile Phrases

We talked in chapter 3 about the most dangerous dating mistakes made by men and how you can avoid them.

This section contains specific phrases you should avoid from your dating profile, except if you don't wish for women to misunderstand or misunderstand you.

#: Ask for any other information.

You should first understand that this phrase is used frequently by women to refer to men in their dating profiles.

It also defeats the purpose of online dating profiles: to get in touch with one another. It can make you look like someone with something to hide, or too lazy to share enough information to spark conversation.

#: "I just got out of a romantic relationship."

If the message you wish to convey is that you are looking for a new relationship, don't include this phrase in your bio. A rebound partner is not something women want.

Worse still, adding this to your bio will tell potential mates, that you aren't done with the relationship and that, as a result, you aren't emotionally stable or available to start anything new.

You should remember, before you use this phrase: 70% of the space should be dedicated in your personal statement to outlining your extraordinary character traits, interests, values etc. and 30% to describing what the character traits and ideals are of the woman that you would like to have in your life.

\#:

The clichés "I hate walking in rain", "I don't like wine under the moonlight," "I don't like long walks on beaches" and "I hate traveling" should be avoided on your dating-profile bio.

These phrases say very little about who you are --most people love the beach or traveling-- and therefore they contraindicate the purpose your bio serves: to let potential partners know who you truly are, your values and what drives your life.

Be more specific and avoid using cliché phrases. Instead of telling people how much you love the beach they should communicate how it makes them feel.

You can also say, "Nothing's as beautiful as watching the sunset over the waters a ocean whose shores are not familiar to me before." This statement shows you love traveling, as well as the best thing about going to the beach.

#:

This phrase can also read as, "I desire a partner whom is loving, generous, kind, hardworking...". Here's the catch: she will be thinking "blah,blah and blah" as she reads this.

Although it is okay to use your bio as a way to talk about the traits and values that you are looking for, this will not be a bad idea. However, making a list of the qualities you seek in a partner is a sign that you are searching for the ideal partner.

3 Additional Online Dating Mistakes you Should Avoid

Be aware of these other mistakes when profile-dating.

#: Vague and general language

You don't communicate your personality or values by using phrases like "funloving, honest. smart." This is a huge mistake.

Keep in mind that the purpose of your bio and description, especially when it comes crafting them, is to give women an idea what values and character traits make you attractive and which will draw you to a partner.

#: You are using the wrong profile pictures

Many sections of this guidebook, including the section about how to create an irresistible on-line dating profile -- have spoken deeply about the importance to have good profile images.

Avoiding using flattering pictures, using profile pictures that don't show women your lifestyle and not using all your available photographs are common mistakes.

#: Not messaging in enough, messaging too often before setting up an appointment

Remember, once you match with a girl it is essential to message her. Don't hesitate to do so!

Keep in mind that online conversations are more likely to go stale when you only talk, chat, and talk some further. It is important to have a friendly, open, playful conversation with her.

Now that you're aware of which errors to avoid in order for women to understand you, let us move on to the next section. This chapter will cover what you need to do to secure a date.

Chapter 20: You are Not Always A Picnic.

Criticism should be treated as a two way street.

This book contains a lot of tips that will help you communicate your criticisms in a positive way. However, that's only half. The second half of this book is about how to open up to criticism, accept it, and take the constructive elements out to learn.

Trust me, she will have similar issues with you just as you had with your lady. There are many reasons she may not have spoken to you: she is not emotional communicative, she doesn't want to hurt anyone's feelings, she is not confrontational, but they still exist and cause resentment.

If you feel strong enough and capable of handling the consequences, it is a good idea to push her to speak up. Asking her about what she thinks of something you did can help you get to the bottom of it.

We all know women don't communicate as naturally or easily with each other. Therefore, you will need to probe her thoughts about a subject. Doubly so for negativities.

It is essential that she feels that her negative thoughts are heard and not just dismissed. To accomplish this, you need to let her know that it is okay to talk to you about things, that your feelings won't be hurt or that you'll regret it later, and that you don't want to get mad.

It can be difficult to implement criticism effectively, but this is an important step in building a relationship that both parties respect each other.

It is me that feels," not you don't.

Sometimes, being a dating and relationship coach is simply about allowing people to process the same emotions in a different context.

This is the delicate interplaying of arguments with your female partner. Even though you may have a valid point, communicating it in a way that your woman can process it and understand it is a mistake.

French, if your Russian wife is French.

The best way to spin something about your woman that is bothering you is to focus on how it affects you, rather than what she is doing. You see a pattern here?

It is important to focus on the effects of her actions instead of the actions. It doesn't discuss the wrongness of her actions or accuse of her being a jackass (even though she might be being one). This is significant for many reasons.

First, she doesn't feel so attacked that he would otherwise. This keeps him open to your needs. She doesn't have immediate defenses or walls.

Second, it emphasizes how you care more about solving a problem that just complaining.

Third, the focus is on improving rather than talking about the present.

Finally, it stops the blame game by implicitly accepting some responsibility. It keeps her nondefensive.

Instead of saying "You aren't washing the dishes enough, what is your problem?" you can say "I feel as though you expect me o wash the dishes after cooking all that time and that makes my life feel really unappreciated."

Your woman will show compassion and empathy if you have any.

"That sounded a lot better in my mind ..."

You have an argument with your woman over whether or not she enjoys spending time with your friends. This sounds familiar enough?

It is possible that your woman doesn't want drama, and is very logical. Are her friends irrational? Or do they have logical reasons not to like them or make it a priority for her to spend time with them?

Do you think there might be an logical explanation for her response?

This is how you can tell the difference between inner intention and external action.

Your actions are not always indicative of your inner thoughts and intent. It's an easy distinction but difficult to grasp and use.

There are many ways to approach this issue. But here's my suggestion: How should you approach your woman in a disagreement?

First, ask yourself if your woman has any intentions of making you mad. It is unlikely that she intends to make you mad or hurt you, so this is a good base. In order to deal with and overcome emotional issues, it's important to differentiate pain and emotion from the root cause.

Second, is she logical at all? If so, give her the benefit of doubt and credit that she actually thought through his decision and can provide some reasoning. Are you more likely to think there was a miscommunication than that your woman wanted your friends to embarrass and humiliate you until you want to fall into the ground like an Ostrich?

Try to imagine what her logic was at that moment. Her inner intentions, though almost always positive, can sometimes be lost in translation to external action.

You don't want to be the one who puts your woman in the doghouse. Take a deep breath, and remember that she will always do what is best for you. While the dishwasher might not be the most romantic gift for an anniversary, she may have noticed your dry hands from washing the dishes all day.

I tend to live strongly by principle of matter. When I realize that my inner intentions are positive and pure, I find it much easier to accept or enjoy any outer action.

Attract her attention to your true self.

People like to think of themselves in certain terms and will stick to their beliefs and fight tooth & nail to preserve them.

If you challenge someone about that perception, you are essentially challenging the person on their identity. That is something you should never do lightly and is always cause for defensiveness.

For example, let's say that you pride yourself in emotional intelligence and empathy. Then someone accuses u of being insensitive towards someone's needs. Your gut reaction is likely to be either denial or strongly negative. This will leave you feeling hurt and questioning yourself.

It can be scary to see something that is very important to us being challenged. This situation can lead to either growth or destruction.

However, when we appeal to something central to ourselves, it is a subtle affirmation for our self-image that has been so hard cultivated... and we will indulge as much as possible. It feels good when we are right about ourselves and others. And it's a great feeling to be able for others to recognize it.

Let's bring all this back to the real world and show our woman what it means.

When she can identify with something she is good and passionate about, she will do things that further strengthen that identity.

Broken down even more, if she thinks she is crafty, and if you appeal to that sense and are good with your hands, you can make her fix things around house and crochet doilies. That will keep her perception.

"Honey Honey, I know your skill and ability to fix things yourself is valuable. Could you please take a look at my squeaky front door when I'm not at work?"

Your woman will be first flattered and feminine. After that, you will feel compelled towards living up to your self-perception.

You'll feel better at it the more you master it. It's okay to throw the pesky m (anipulation) word out with the wind. Because identity is a very painful thing to give up and let go.

You can even appeal directly to the person you want to be. It will actually make them want more to share and confirm their perception.

Understanding her physical reactions is key.

Let's just say, it's not the fault of anyone if they can't control what happens to their bodies. There is no need to feel guilty or ashamed for looking less than perfect. They are only a reflection inside of us, and not a positive or negative trait.

This chapter doesn't aim to discredit anyone or force people to stop feeling like robots.

This chapter will simply explain the meaning of your woman's physical reactions, and how you may feel compelled by them to react.

I am primarily referring here to her crying and tears. You'll feel very strong emotions when you start crying in many situations, conversations and with your woman. Tears are a great way to get out of your pain and help stop it from continuing.

You will want your daughter to be comforted, taken care of, and assured that all will be well. You will be there to hug and stroke her hair as you point out the happier things, like rainbows and puppies.

This is to suggest that most men are not well-equipped to handle the crying of a woman.

This is very sweet of us. However, it is going to either distract from the issue or make it worse. Either it will be a distraction that merely pacifies the situation, or it will magnify it and make us believe it was more important than it is.

Other physical reactions she might have include an inadvertently raised voice, closing down physically and posturally as well as sniffling, anger gestures, and so on.

It isn't something men can do. However, understanding the consequences and emotions of their physical reactions can help us to understand the larger picture and the feelings of each side during an argument or conversation.

Conclusion

It may seem that some men have it all, but you find yourself facing challenges that you can't overcome. Some men are able to make it work because they know what they're supposed to say. Learning to appear charming, smooth, and charming is more important than being creepy or awkward. A foolproof system is essential to ensure that you never lose your chance with potential lovers. With some guidance, your relationship can be transformed.

Your attitude towards dating must be changed. A lot of men believe that it's easy to find love. These thoughts should be challenged. You have to change your perception of yourself and women. It is important to have a positive mindset and be confident. Now all you have to do is implement the tips in this book.

www.ingramcontent.com/pod-product-compliance
Lightning Source LLC
Chambersburg PA
CBHW050402120526
44590CB00015B/1791